Jesus
Man of Pr

A Guided Discovery for Groups and Individuals
Kevin Perrotta

LOYOLA PRESS.
A JESUIT MINISTRY
Chicago

LOYOLA PRESS.
A JESUIT MINISTRY

3441 N. Ashland Avenue
Chicago, Illinois 60657
(800) 621-1008
www.loyolapress.com

Nihil Obstat	*Imprimatur*
Reverend John G. Lodge, SSL, STD	Reverend John F. Canary, STL, DMin
Censor Deputatus	Vicar General
November 7, 2006	Archdiocese of Chicago
	November 8, 2006

The *Nihil Obstat* and *Imprimatur* are official declarations that a book is free of doctrinal and moral error. No implication is contained therein that those who have granted the *Nihil Obstat* and *Imprimatur* agree with the content, opinions, or statements expressed. Nor do they assume any legal responsibility associated with publication.

Unless otherwise noted, the Scripture quotations contained herein are from the New Revised Standard Version Bible: Catholic Edition, copyright © 1993 and 1989 by the Division of Christian Education of the National Council of the Churches of Christ in the U.S.A. Used by permission. All rights reserved. Subheadings in Scripture quotations have been added by Kevin Perrotta.

The translation of the quotation from Origen, *On First Principles*, 2:6:2, on page 9, is taken from Thomas C. Oden and Christopher A. Hall, *Mark*, Ancient Christian Commentary on Scripture, vol. 2 (Downers Grove, IL: InterVarsity Press, 1998), 209.

The excerpt from the autobiography of St. Thérèse of Lisieux, *The Story of a Soul*, on page 45, is adapted from the translation by Thomas Taylor for the Project Gutenberg e-book edition (www.gutenberg.org).

The excerpt from a prayer by Francis Xavier Nguyen Van Thuan, on page 71, is taken from his book *Five Loaves and Two Fish* (Boston: Pauline Books & Media, 2003), 12–14.

The words of Blessed John XXIII quoted on page 83 are excerpted from Peter Hebblethwaite, *Pope John XXIII: Shepherd of the Modern World* (Garden City, NY: Doubleday & Company, 1985), 501–2.

Interior design by Kay Hartmann/Communique Design
Illustration by Anni Betts

ISBN-13: 978-0-8294-2327-3; ISBN-10: 0-8294-2327-3

Printed in the United States of America
11 12 13 14 15 16 Bang 10 9 8 7 6 5 4 3 2

Contents

How to Use This Guide

You might compare the Bible to a national park. The park is so large that you could spend months, even years, getting to know it. But a brief visit, if carefully planned, can be enjoyable and worthwhile. In a few hours you can drive through the park and pull over at a handful of sites. At each stop you can get out of the car, take a short trail through the woods, listen to the wind blowing through the trees, get a feel for the place.

In this book, we will read sections of the Gospels that show us Jesus in prayer. Because the excerpts are short, we will be able to take a leisurely walk through them, thinking carefully about Jesus' prayer and what it means for us.

This guide provides everything you need to explore the Gospel excerpts in six discussions—or to do a six-part exploration on your own. The introduction on page 6 will prepare you to get the most out of your reading. The weekly sections provide explanations that will help illuminate the meanings of the readings for your life. Equally important, each section supplies questions that will launch your group into fruitful discussion, helping you to both investigate the Scripture readings for yourself and learn from one another. If you're using the book by yourself, the questions will spur your personal reflection.

Each discussion is meant to be a *guided discovery*.

Guided. None of us is equipped to read the Bible without help. We read the Bible *for* ourselves but not *by* ourselves. Scripture was written to be understood and applied in the community of faith. So each week you'll find background and explanations in "A Guide to the Reading," which draws on the work of both modern biblical scholars and Christian writers of the past. The guide will help you grasp the meanings of Gospel readings. Think of it as a friendly park ranger who points out noteworthy details and explains what you're looking at so you can appreciate things for yourself.

Discovery. The purpose is for *you* to interact with the biblical readings. "Questions for Careful Reading" is a tool to help you dig into the text and examine it carefully. "Questions for Application" will help you consider what these words mean for your life here and now. Each week concludes with an "Approach to Prayer" section that helps you respond to God's word. Supplementary "Living Tradition" and "Saints in the Making" sections offer the thoughts and experiences of Christians past and present. By showing what Jesus' prayer has meant to others, these sections will help you consider what it means for you. Sections after Week 3 and Week 6 look at two Gospel passages on Jesus' prayer not covered in the weekly sessions.

How long are the discussion sessions? We've assumed you will have about an hour and a half when you get together. If you have less time, you'll find that most of the elements can be shortened somewhat.

Is homework necessary? You will get the most out of your discussions if you read the weekly material and prepare answers to the questions in advance of each meeting. If participants are not able to prepare, have someone read the "Guide to the Reading" sections aloud to the group at the points where they appear.

What about leadership? If you happen to have a world-class biblical scholar in your group, by all means ask him or her to lead the discussions. In the absence of any professional Scripture scholars, or even accomplished amateur biblical scholars, you can still have a first-class Bible discussion. Choose two or three people to take turns as facilitators, and have everyone read "Suggestions for Bible Discussion Groups" (page 92) before beginning.

Does everyone need a guide? a Bible? Everyone in the group will need his or her own copy of this book. It contains all the Gospel excerpts discussed in the weekly sessions, so a Bible is not absolutely necessary—but each participant will find it useful to have one. You should have at least one Bible on hand for your discussions. (See page 96 for recommendations.)

How do we get started? Before you begin, take a look at the suggestions for Bible discussion groups (page 92) or individuals (page 95).

The Blue Thread

In a village in first-century Galilee, a woman suffering from a chronic ailment saw Jesus walking down the street and struggled through a crowd of people to get close to him. The woman was hesitant to introduce herself, but she wanted at least to touch his clothing. She was sure that even indirect contact with Jesus would bring her healing. Coming up behind him, she stretched out her hand to the fringe on his robe—and immediately she felt his healing power. You can read the story in Luke's Gospel (8:43–48).

It is interesting to learn that Jesus' robe had a "fringe" or, perhaps, tassels. This tells us that he followed the common Jewish practice of the time of putting a fringe or tassels on one's outer garment. (Such tassels are still found on the prayer shawls of Jews today.) Woven into the fringe, or tassels, was a sea-blue thread. If a man could afford to have his robe bleached, the blue thread would stand out vividly against the surrounding white fabric. But the blue thread would stand out even against a background of unbleached gray, for blue was rarely seen in clothing, as blue dye was astronomically expensive.

Jewish men, and some Jewish women, ornamented their outer robe this way in obedience to a biblical command. The ornamentation reminded them of God's commandments given to them and his call to them to be holy (Numbers 15:37–41). Since parts of the Jewish high priest's clothing were blue (Exodus 28:6), the blue thread in ordinary Jews' clothing was a token that the whole people of Israel was a priesthood in which every member enjoyed the privilege of standing in God's presence to offer him thanks and praise.

I like to picture Jesus wearing his fringed robe. The white cloth fittingly symbolizes the purity of his love for God and people. The blue thread I take as a symbol of his prayer. Prayer, in fact, ran like a bright thread through the fabric of Jesus' life from beginning to end. When we first hear him speaking in the Gospels, at the age of twelve, he is standing in the Jerusalem temple, Judaism's central place of prayer (Luke 2:41–51). His dying words are fragments of biblical prayers (Mark 15:34; Luke 23:46).

In this book, we will take up the thread of Jesus' prayer from his baptism in the Jordan to his death on Golgotha. Jesus' prayerfulness is a side of his personality that is often neglected. As Christians, we regard Jesus as Lord, Savior, teacher, healer, and bread of life. Our readings will show us that this Lord, who saves, teaches, heals, and feeds us with himself, is also a man of prayer. Observing Jesus in prayer is instructive for our own prayer. There are many men and women in the Christian tradition and in the Church today who can teach us how to pray, but on this subject, Jesus is *the* guide. In this book, we will learn from Jesus about prayer by considering him as our model. We will not read the sections of the Gospels that contain his teaching about prayer, since those instructions deserve separate attention. For a Six Weeks with the Bible book on the heart of Jesus' instructions about prayer, see *Our Father: The Prayer Jesus Taught Us*.

In our readings from the Gospels, we will follow Jesus in a roughly chronological way, observing him praying in various situations that arose after he emerged from the obscurity of Nazareth. In Week 3, however, we will pause in our chronological exploration to consider his customary forms of prayer—how he prayed in the morning, at meals, and on the Sabbath, both before and during his public life.

If we had more than six sessions, we could also look at another aspect of Jesus' customary prayer: his participation in the annual Jewish pilgrimage feasts in Jerusalem (see John 2:13–17; 5:1–18; 7:1–14; 7:53–8:11; 10:22–30). And we could examine other particular occasions on which he prayed (for example, John 11:41–42; 12:27–28). The present book is just a short introduction to Jesus' prayer in the Gospels and cannot explore all these passages. But perhaps it will spur you to explore them yourself.

Prayer being such an obviously spiritual activity, we might expect that Jesus' prayer would especially highlight his divine nature. Yet while Jesus' prayer draws attention to his divine union with his Father, it also highlights the completeness of his sharing in our humanity. Before the Incarnation, the divine

Son offered no prayer to his divine Father. The trinity of divine persons in God—Father, Son, and Holy Spirit—live always in a total communion of love, unrestricted by anything as limited as prayer. It was only when the Son took flesh that prayer became an essential expression of his love for his Father. Thus, simply to look at Jesus in prayer is to be reminded that he is a man, one of us, a member of our human race.

Over and over, Jesus' prayer gives us vivid insights into his humanity. It is notable, for example, that he prays before major undertakings, crucial choices, and significant conversations—as we see in our readings in Weeks 1 and 4. By showing Jesus praying at such pivotal moments, the Gospel writers seem to indicate that he was seeking his Father's will, as would any devout man or woman facing a challenge or critical decision. Of course, here we are touching on a deep mystery. How could the eternal Son, who knew the Father fully, grow in knowledge of his Father's plans? Yet, whatever answer we give to this question, we cannot deny that Jesus grew up and matured in a normal way (Luke 2:40). His wisdom increased over time (Luke 2:52). Presumably, even after he reached adulthood, Jesus continued to grow in understanding of his Father's will. Presumably, prayer played a part in this growth.

Jesus' humanity is also on display in his prayer at times of difficulty and distress. As we watch him dealing with temptations at the beginning of his public life (one of our readings in Week 1) and facing his suffering and death before his arrest (Week 5), we realize that, even though he is the divine Son of the Father, he feels the needs and desires that all humans experience. We see clearly that, while Jesus is totally obedient to his Father, he has a will of his own. He makes human choices to live as the obedient Son of God—and the choosing is not always easy for him. His eternal bond with the Father is never diminished, yet he must decide to place his human desires and will in his Father's hands. Like us, Jesus maintains his trust in his Father and his obedience to the Father only with some degree of struggle. And, as in our lives, the struggle is played out in prayer. Of all Jesus' prayers, his last one gives the most astounding evidence of his humanity (our reading in Week 6). As he dies on the cross, Jesus expresses to his Father his profound grief at being abandoned to the power of his tormenters. The deep mystery of the divine Son's humanity demonstrated in Jesus' dying prayer led Origen, a great Egyptian theologian of the third century, to remark:

When we see in him some things so human that they appear in no way to differ from the common frailty of mortals, and some things so divine that they are appropriate to nothing else but the primal and ineffable nature of deity, the human understanding with its own narrow limits is baffled, and struck with amazement at so mighty a wonder.

As we read about Jesus man of prayer, it is important to keep both sides of the paradox of his divine and human natures in view. The Gospel writers often tell us that Jesus prayed, but they rarely give us information about the content of his prayer. They seem to imply that the prayerful communion of the divine Son with the Father is a mystery into which we may not intrude. Presumably, in his prayer, Jesus experienced incomprehensible union with his Father. Yet the aspects of Jesus' prayer that the Gospel writers *do* show us reveal his thoroughly human qualities: devotion, joy, fear, perseverance, courage, grief. Thus, perhaps unexpectedly, Jesus seems especially close to us when he is praying, even though the inner reality of his prayer—the infinite love of the eternal Son for the eternal Father—is hidden from our eyes.

The combination of divine and human dimensions in Jesus is expressed very simply and profoundly in the way he characteristically addressed God: he called him "Father." By taking the position of Son speaking to his Father, Jesus gave us the deepest metaphor, drawn from common human experience, for understanding the relationship between the first and second persons of the Trinity: they are like Father and Son. No human concept can enable us to comprehend the inner life of God. But in his prayers recorded in the Gospels, Jesus gives us "Father" and

"Son" as the most precious and revealing terms by which we can know these persons of the Trinity.

At the same time, could any term for God be more resonantly human and down-to-earth than *Father*? There is a totally human tone of reverence, affection, obedience, and trust in Jesus' address to God as "Father." The Jesus who addresses God as Father is no partly incarnated divine being merely wearing a mask of flesh. As he prays to God as Father, we glimpse Jesus' heart and see that it is as human as ours. His prayer shows him to be a man like us—a person whose divine nature has taken on our humanity in every respect.

This point is especially prominent in Mark's account of Jesus' prayer in Gethsemane before he dies (Mark 14:36). Mark, who writes in Greek, leaves untranslated the Aramaic word that Jesus, a native Aramaic speaker, used in his prayer: *Abba*, that is, "Father!" This Aramaic word reminds us that, like every one of us, Jesus lived in a particular time and place, belonged to a particular culture, spoke a particular language, and experienced particular desires, fears, sorrows, and joys.

Jesus gave his first disciples the opportunity to be with him as he prayed. Through the Gospels, he extends that opportunity to us. To take advantage of it, we need to complete our process of reading, reflection, and discussion with prayer. I hope that as you observe Jesus praying in the Gospel readings, you will take time to be alone with him and speak to him about prayer. In prayer, each of us can reach out to him, as did the woman in the Gospel story. Stretch out your finger to Jesus' robe, touch the blue thread of prayer running through his life, and experience his life-creating power, his love for his Father.

Lord Jesus,
Son of the Father
and Son of Mary,
thank you for all your prayers—
in Nazareth
and in Jerusalem,
on lonely hilltops
and with your disciples,
in synagogues and in the temple,
in moments of anguish
and of joy.
Praise to you for incarnating
    your love for the Father
in this human way.
Lord Jesus, as we read the
    Gospel accounts of your
    prayer—
and pray in response to these
    readings—
lead us more deeply
into your Father's love.

TRUE SON OF HIS FATHER

Questions to Begin

15 minutes
Use a question or two to get warmed up for the reading.

1 What is one trait or habit—large or small—that you're happy you picked up from your mother or father?

2 When was the last time you made a major new start in life?

Opening the Bible

5 minutes
Read the passage aloud. Let individuals take turns reading
paragraphs.

The Background

In two excerpts from Luke's Gospel, we see Jesus making the transition from private to public life. In the first reading, Jesus has traveled from his hometown, Nazareth, in the hill country of Galilee, down to the place along the Jordan River where a prophet named John—commonly called "the Baptist"—has been calling on people to repent of their sins. John expects that God will soon bring judgment on the world; he offers to baptize people as a sign of their repentance and preparation for God's coming. Jesus is sinless, but he accepts baptism from John as a token of his approval of John's call to repentance—even though Jesus has come to bring God's forgiveness rather than immediate judgment. The episode in our second reading occurs immediately after Jesus' baptism. Jesus goes into the barren region near the Jordan River for a time of solitude before beginning his ministry of teaching, healing, and gathering disciples.

The Reading: Luke 3:21–22; 4:1–14

Prayer at the River

3:21 Now when all the people were baptized, and when Jesus also had been baptized and was praying, the heaven was opened, 22 and the Holy Spirit descended upon him in bodily form like a dove. And a voice came from heaven, "You are my Son, the Beloved; with you I am well pleased."

Prayer in the Wilderness

4:1 Jesus, full of the Holy Spirit, returned from the Jordan and was led by the Spirit in the wilderness, 2 where for forty days he was tempted by the devil. He ate nothing at all during those days, and when they were over, he was famished.

3 The devil said to him, "If you are the Son of God, command this stone to become a loaf of bread."

⁴ Jesus answered him, "It is written, 'One does not live by bread alone.'"

⁵ Then the devil led him up and showed him in an instant all the kingdoms of the world. ⁶ And the devil said to him, "To you I will give their glory and all this authority; for it has been given over to me, and I give it to anyone I please. ⁷ If you, then, will worship me, it will all be yours."

⁸ Jesus answered him, "It is written, 'Worship the Lord your God, and serve only him.'"

⁹ Then the devil took him to Jerusalem, and placed him on the pinnacle of the temple, saying to him, "If you are the Son of God, throw yourself down from here, ¹⁰ for it is written, 'He will command his angels concerning you, to protect you,' ¹¹ and 'On their hands they will bear you up, so that you will not dash your foot against a stone.'"

¹² Jesus answered him, "It is said, 'Do not put the Lord your God to the test.'"

¹³ When the devil had finished every test, he departed from him until an opportune time.

¹⁴ Then Jesus, filled with the power of the Spirit, returned to Galilee, and a report about him spread through all the surrounding country.

10 minutes
Choose questions according to your interest and time.

1 The dove in Luke 3:22 was visible: (1) only to Jesus, (2) only to the people around him, (3) to both, (4) can't tell.

2 In Luke 4:8–12 the Devil and Jesus both quote Scripture. Do they have different ways of interpreting Scripture?

3 During his public ministry, Jesus uses his divine power to drive the Devil away from people (4:33–35; 8:1–2, 26–39). When the Devil tempts Jesus, why doesn't Jesus just drive him away?

4 From Luke 4:1–13, or other passages in the Gospels, would you say that it was easy for Jesus to resist temptations?

5 Jesus quotes Scripture in Luke 4:4, 8, 12. Does he direct his quotations to the Devil or to himself?

6 What is Jesus' strategy for overcoming temptation? Does he use any power not available to the rest of us to overcome temptations?

A Guide to the Reading

If participants have not read this section already, read it aloud. Otherwise go on to "Questions for Application."

3:21–22. Because he is God's Son, Jesus is filled with the Holy Spirit from the beginning of his human life. Yet as he goes through stages of growth and comes to turning points and crises (see 2:40, 52), the Spirit becomes active in him in new ways. Here we see the Father giving Jesus the Spirit more deeply to empower him for the work he is about to begin.

Along with this outpouring of the Spirit, the Father gives Jesus an assurance of his affection and approval: "You are my Son, the Beloved; with you I am well pleased." God does not speak to Jesus about his mission but about their relationship with each other, which is the foundation of the mission. It is only because Jesus is God's Son that he will be able to reconcile men and women to God.

The renewed gift of the Spirit and the Father's words of love come to Jesus as he prays. This suggests the importance of prayer in his relationship with his Father. Jesus knows the Father continuously in the depths of his being, yet this knowledge does not make prayer unnecessary for him. In fact, here we see that prayer is a special occasion for Jesus to experience his divine sonship and his sharing in the Spirit.

4:1–2. As the divine Son, Jesus knows his mission. As a man, however, he may well need to reflect on the nature of that mission—and its personal cost—before setting out on it. Jesus' fasting is a clue that reflection on his mission is a reason for his time in the wilderness, since fasting is an aid to discerning God's will and preparing for action (Acts 13:1–3). Luke does not mention prayer during Jesus' forty-day retreat, but it goes without saying that this was a time of prayer.

Although Luke does not say so explicitly, we may well believe that Jesus' prayer after his baptism was a moment of exaltation. Yet his prayer in the wilderness does not seem to be saturated in glory. Over a period of six weeks, Jesus struggles against temptations to turn away from his Father: "For forty days he was tempted by the devil" (4:2). We may assume that the temptations are as real for Jesus as his hunger pangs. Each of the temptations contains something that he might find appealing. At the same time, however, we must admit that we touch on a mystery here. For while Scripture speaks of Jesus being tempted, it makes it clear that there was no sin in him (Hebrews 4:15). As the Son of God and the perfect human being, Jesus experienced absolutely none of the tendency toward sin that we experience as a consequence of original sin. In any case, without trying to comprehend Jesus' inner experience of his temptations, we can learn a great deal by observing how he handles them.

On one level, the temptations touch on issues concerning how Jesus will conduct his ministry. Will he use flashy miracles that pander to people's earthly desires (the first temptation)? Will he employ military and political power to achieve his ends (the third)? At a deeper level, the temptations touch on his relationship with God. Each temptation poses the question "Will you, or will you not, live your human life as the loving, faithful, trusting Son of your Father?"

A side note: it is probably futile to try to determine what the Devil knows or doesn't know about Jesus. The only evidence of the Devil's thinking is his own words, and he is not committed to expressing his thoughts truthfully. He says whatever serves his purposes. His quoting of Scripture, for example, does not indicate that he believes God's word; on the contrary, he quotes Scripture in order to cast a doubt on it (4:9–11).

4:3–4. In the first temptation, the Devil proposes that Jesus transform a stone into a loaf of bread. Jesus might well be inclined to do exactly that, since he hasn't eaten for weeks. In response, however, Jesus quotes Scripture: "One does not live by bread alone" (4:4). This statement appears in the book of Deuteronomy, where it is followed by the words "but by every word that comes from the mouth of the Lord" (Deuteronomy 8:3). The Deuteronomy passage is discussing the Israelites' travels in the wilderness, during which they treated earthly bread as more important than the "bread" of knowing and doing God's will. Jesus refuses to make this mistake. He gives top priority to God's word. As we know, the Father just recently said to Jesus, "You are my Son" (3:22). *This* is the word on which Jesus lives (see John 4:32–34).

Why would it be contrary to his Father's will for Jesus to turn a stone into a loaf of bread? Soon Jesus will miraculously bring many loaves of bread into existence (9:12–17). Here, however, Jesus is urged to use his extraordinary power *for himself*: "If you are the Son of God, command this stone to become a loaf of bread," the Devil says, assuming that anyone who possesses extraordinary powers will use them for his or her own benefit. But because Jesus *is* the Son of God, he will *not* use his miraculous powers to satisfy himself. Being God's Son does not mean being in the position of directing everything to his own benefit. Quite the contrary. Divine sonship is a matter not of grasping but of giving—of self-giving love (Philippians 2:6–8). Jesus expresses his divine sonship by being totally focused on carrying out his Father's plans for the good of his fellow human beings, by using his extraordinary powers not for himself but for others. From the beginning to the end of his ministry, Jesus never works a miracle solely for his own benefit. He refuses to serve himself.

By refraining from using his extraordinary powers to make his own life easy, Jesus remains within the limitations of the human condition. Only in this way can he be a model for us, who lack miraculous powers.

4:5–8. The second temptation is to have earthly rule and its advantages. In his response to the Devil, Jesus does not indicate that he thinks that earthly power is wrong. And, obviously, Jesus would make an excellent ruler. Nevertheless, he refuses the Devil's offer. To gain this power, he would have to worship the Devil. If satisfying a desire or attaining a goal involves total devotion to anyone or anything besides God, Jesus rejects it.

The heart of Jesus' mission will be to make God known and loved, to establish God's kingdom—God's rule—in people's lives. Jesus has come to lead us out of the rebellion of sin and into an acceptance of God's fatherly love and will for our lives. Here we see that he promotes this way of living by living this way himself.

4:9–13. What is the nature of the third temptation? Is Jesus being tempted to display himself as the Messiah by flying through the air? Perhaps, although flying through the air was not an expected sign of the Messiah, so it might not convince people of his messiahship.

In fact, however, the Devil does not suggest to Jesus that he fly. He suggests that Jesus throw himself from the top of the wall around the temple and give God a chance to fulfill his promise of protection contained in Psalm 91. A person who doubts God's trustworthiness might feel tempted to resolve his or her doubts by putting God's promises to the test. Thus, the temptation here is for Jesus to satisfy any doubts he may have about God. As in the first temptation, the Devil poses this one with the words "If you are the Son of God." Apparently, the Devil assumes that every human being—even one who is especially close to God—would have doubts about God's faithfulness.

As the eternal Son, Jesus could not doubt his Father's faithfulness. But perhaps, in his human nature, he could be assailed by such a temptation (see St. Ambrose's comment on Jesus' final prayer on page 76). But Jesus rejects the suggestion of putting God's promises to the test. In Jesus' view, God's promises to human beings are an invitation to trust God. To use one of God's promises as a tool for probing God's trustworthiness would be the very opposite of faith in God.

At the Jordan River, the Father declared that he was well pleased with the Son. In the wilderness, the Son has now demonstrated that he is totally dedicated to the Father. Luke has not described the inner dimensions of Jesus' prayer in the desert—the words he spoke to his Father, the manner in which he experienced the Father's love, or the movement of the Spirit within him. Rather, Luke has shown us Jesus resisting every temptation to depart from faithfulness to his Father. In the wilderness, Jesus declines to satisfy his own needs but insists on putting his entire strength into doing his Father's will. He refuses to shift his devotion to anything or anyone besides his Father. He resists any doubt about his Father's faithfulness and love. Thus Luke has shown us the bedrock on which Jesus stood in prayer: his love for his Father.

Questions for Application

40 minutes
Choose questions according to your interest and time.

1 Reread Luke 3:21. When *you* pray, does heaven seem to open up? Have there been moments in prayer when you have felt especially close to God? If so, what impact have these experiences had on you? How important—or unimportant—are such moments for a person's relationship with God?

2 Besides praying the Our Father, do you pray to God as your Father? Why or why not?

3 How important is prayer in getting to know God?

4 At present, are you making some new start in life? If so, how could you seek the presence and power of the Holy Spirit for this new beginning?

5 Have you ever taken a retreat to seek God's guidance and help for the next stage in your life? If so, what did it accomplish? Would you do it again?

6 What are your temptations to use your talents and resources for yourself rather than for others? How could you direct some ability or resource of yours toward serving someone else's needs?

7 What is the situation in which you are most tempted to doubt God's love for you? How could you affirm your trust in God in this situation?

8 How do this week's readings give you a deeper understanding of Jesus?

9 What encouragement or guidance for your own prayer do you find in Jesus' prayer in this week's readings? How will you respond?

Approach to Prayer

15 minutes
Use this approach—or create your own!

+ The Devil quotes Psalm 91 to
  Jesus (Luke 4:10–11) to stir up
  doubts about God. Pray Psalm
  91 together as an expression
  of trust in God. Pause for silent
  reflection. End with a Glory to
  the Father.

A Living Tradition

Calling On the Spirit

This section is a supplement for individual reading.

The Holy Spirit descended on Jesus at his baptism. Jesus urges us, his followers, to seek the coming of the Holy Spirit (Luke 24:49; Acts 1:4–5). To help you in seeking the Spirit, here are three prayers widely used by Christians in the Byzantine tradition.

A hymn to the Holy Spirit

O Holy Spirit,
    Mighty defender,
To all who love you
    Comfort you give.
Everywhere present,
    Fountain of virtues,
Without your kindness,
    No one could live.

O Holy Spirit,
    Treasury of blessings,
Come, as was promised,
    Life-giving flame.
Come, dwell within us,
    Quicken our cool hearts,
Strengthen our purpose
    To praise your name.

Prayers to the Holy Spirit at the beginning of work

O God, author and creator of all things,
With your blessing guide this work,
Which is being undertaken for your glory.
Deliver us from every evil,
For you alone are almighty
And love mankind.

O Lord, you are prompt to defend
And mighty in your help.
Be present now through the grace of your power.
Bless us and give us strength
And bring to completion
The intentions of your servants to do good works,
For you can, as the Almighty God,
Do everything you wish.

WORK AND PRAY

Questions to Begin

15 minutes
Use a question or two to get warmed up for the reading.

1   How early do you like to get up in the morning? How late do you like to go to bed?

2   How easy is it for you to find a time and place to be by yourself for prayer?

5 minutes
Read the passage aloud. Let individuals take turns reading
paragraphs.

What's Happened

Once he begins his public ministry, Jesus no longer makes extended
retreats. Instead of going into the desert for weeks at a time, he
takes shorter prayer breaks in nearby deserted places. This week,
we see him seeking solitude soon after he begins his ministry and
again sometime later.

The Reading: Mark 1:21, 23–26, 29–39; 6:30–51

One Busy Day

1:21 They went to Capernaum; and when the sabbath came, he
entered the synagogue and taught. . . . 23 Just then there was in their
synagogue a man with an unclean spirit, 24 and he cried out, "What
have you to do with us, Jesus of Nazareth? Have you come to destroy
us? I know who you are, the Holy One of God." 25 But Jesus rebuked
him, saying, "Be silent, and come out of him!" 26 And the unclean
spirit, convulsing him and crying with a loud voice, came out of
him. . . .

29 As soon as they left the synagogue, they entered the house
of Simon and Andrew, with James and John. 30 Now Simon's
mother-in-law was in bed with a fever, and they told him about her
at once. 31 He came and took her by the hand and lifted her up. Then
the fever left her, and she began to serve them.

32 That evening, at sundown, they brought to him all who
were sick or possessed with demons. 33 And the whole city was
gathered around the door. 34 And he cured many who were sick with
various diseases, and cast out many demons. . . .

35 In the morning, while it was still very dark, he got up and
went out to a deserted place, and there he prayed. 36 And Simon and
his companions hunted for him.

37 When they found him, they said to him, "Everyone is
searching for you." 38 He answered, "Let us go on to the neighboring
towns, so that I may proclaim the message there also; for that is what
I came out to do." 39 And he went throughout Galilee, proclaiming
the message in their synagogues and casting out demons.

Busier and Busier

6:30 The apostles gathered around Jesus, and . . . 31 he said to them, "Come away to a deserted place all by yourselves and rest a while." For many were coming and going, and they had no leisure even to eat. 32 And they went away in the boat to a deserted place by themselves. 33 Now many saw them going and recognized them, and they hurried there on foot from all the towns and arrived ahead of them. 34 As he went ashore, he saw a great crowd; and he had compassion for them, because they were like sheep without a shepherd; and he began to teach them many things. 35 When it grew late, his disciples came to him and said, "This is a deserted place, and the hour is now very late; 36 send them away so that they may go into the surrounding country and villages and buy something for themselves to eat." 37 But he answered them, "You give them something to eat." They said to him, "Are we to go and buy two hundred denarii worth of bread, and give it to them to eat?" 38 And he said to them, "How many loaves have you? Go and see." When they had found out, they said, "Five, and two fish." 39 Then he ordered them to get all the people to sit down in groups on the green grass. 40 So they sat down in groups of hundreds and of fifties. 41 Taking the five loaves and the two fish, he looked up to heaven, and blessed and broke the loaves, and gave them to his disciples to set before the people; and he divided the two fish among them all. 42 And all ate and were filled; 43 and they took up twelve baskets full of broken pieces and of the fish. 44 Those who had eaten the loaves numbered five thousand men.

45 Immediately he made his disciples get into the boat and go on ahead to the other side, to Bethsaida, while he dismissed the crowd. 46 After saying farewell to them, he went up on the mountain to pray.

47 When evening came, the boat was out on the sea, and he was alone on the land. 48 When he saw that they were straining at the oars against an adverse wind, he came towards them early in the morning, walking on the sea. He intended to pass them by. 49 But when they saw him walking on the sea, they thought it was a ghost and cried out; 50 for they all saw him and were terrified. But immediately he spoke to them and said, "Take heart, it is I; do not be afraid." 51 Then he got into the boat with them and the wind ceased.

10 minutes
Choose questions according to your interest and time.

1 Whose house does Jesus enter in Mark 1:29–30?

2 Why do the disciples tell Jesus what they tell him in Mark 1:37? What does their statement imply about what they think he should do and the kind of ministry he should have? What might their statement imply about why they have become Jesus' disciples?

3 How would you describe the tone of the disciples' question to Jesus in Mark 6:37?

4 Scholars puzzle over why Jesus sends the disciples away before saying good-bye to the crowd (6:45–46). What do you think is his reason?

5 It has been suggested by some who have difficulty accepting miracles that Jesus was actually wading in shallow water when the disciples saw him (6:48–50). How much sense does this explanation make? Base your response on details given in the Gospel account.

A Guide to the Reading

If participants have not read this section already, read it aloud. Otherwise go on to "Questions for Application."

1:21–39. The Sabbath is a day of rest, but Jesus works hard on the Sabbath that Mark recounts here. Jesus teaches and performs a healing during the synagogue service; then, at Simon's home, he performs another healing and spends the rest of the day with his disciples—more teaching, we can be sure. At sundown, when the Sabbath ends, neighbors crowd into the house, hoping for more healings. Jesus probably has a late night. Yet the next morning, he does not sleep in but gets up very early to go off by himself to pray. He probably expects another busy day—and is determined that it will not be a prayerless one.

The disciples track Jesus down and tell him, "Everyone is searching for you." The people of Capernaum want him to stay on and give them the benefits of a residential healer. But this is not Jesus' plan (1:38). Despite pressures from his disciples and the townspeople, he will keep to his own agenda. Mark has not told us about the content of Jesus' morning prayer. But we can get some sense of it by noticing that he has emerged from it with a clear sense of God's purpose for him and a determination not to be deflected from it.

6:30–51. After many busy days, the disciples are tired and, presumably, so is Jesus. But the crowd of people seeking—almost demanding—healing makes it impossible for them to sit down for a meal. Jesus suggests to the disciples that they sail to a quieter place along the lakeshore to relax (6:31). But a crowd numbering in the thousands (6:44) figures out where they are headed and gets there first.

Jesus and the crowd are so centered on his teaching that they do not notice time passing. No one is thinking about eating—except the disciples. *Their* attention wanders from Jesus' teaching to the meal and rest that they have been looking forward to. They advise Jesus to send the crowd away (6:35–36)—a reasonable suggestion, to which Jesus makes an apparently unreasonable response: "You give them something to eat" (6:37). But then, to enable the disciples to do it, he performs a miracle. The crowd does not seem to grasp what is happening. Jesus has apparently designed the miracle especially for the disciples: a lesson in caring for others even when they prefer peace and quiet.

Yet Jesus also appreciates peace and quiet. He brusquely sends the disciples away. Then he dismisses the crowd—thus giving the disciples what they wished for ("send them away"—6:36), but not in the way they wished! The disciples have missed their day off, and there is little prospect of their getting a rest in well-populated Bethsaida (6:45). Alone at last, Jesus goes up a nearby hill to pray. Not mere duty but longing and love would impel Jesus to find time for such prayer at the end of an exhausting day.

Now follows a strange scene. The disciples have set out at sunset, but they are still on the lake "early in the morning." The lake is only six or seven miles across, so they have been making very slow progress. Apparently they have run into a severe storm. If Jesus, up on the hill, is praying with his eyes open, as people did in those days, perhaps he is watching the disciples struggling against the wind and waves and is praying for them.

Eventually Jesus comes down from the hill and walks out over the lake. He does not intend to rescue the disciples (they don't seem to be in danger) but to "pass them by" (6:48). Readers who know their Old Testament may be reminded of the scene in which God revealed himself to Moses by passing by him (Exodus 33:17–34:8). Thus it seems that the purpose of Jesus' appearance to the disciples on the lake is to give them a glimpse of his divinity in the midst of the storm. Jesus underlines his self-revealing purpose by calling out, "It is I" (6:50), which is a form of self-identification used by God in Scripture (see Exodus 3:14; Isaiah 41:4; 43:10–11).

Jesus' revelation of his divinity to his disciples on the lake seems to overflow from his prayer as a reflection of the intimacy and intensity of the communion with his Father that he has just been experiencing on the hill.

Questions for Application

40 minutes
Choose questions according to your interest and time.

1 In these readings, what obstacles to prayer did Jesus face? Are his obstacles to prayer anything like yours?

2 Most days, what opportunities for solitude do you have? Do you use these opportunities for prayer?

3 Reread Mark 1:29–30. If Jesus were to make a special visit to your home, what would you talk to him about?

4 How does prayer help you perceive God's agenda for your life and stay with it?

5 Did the disciples grasp the revelation of himself that Jesus offered them in the storm? If God tried to reveal himself to you while you were changing a tire in a rainstorm or while you were pacing the bedroom with a cranky baby in the middle of the night, would you notice? Can God make himself present in turbulent and confusing situations? Have you ever had this kind of experience?

6 How do this week's readings give you a deeper understanding of Jesus?

7 What encouragement or guidance for your own prayer do you find in Jesus' prayer in this week's readings? How will you respond?

Approach to Prayer

15 minutes
Use one of these approaches—or create your own!

♦ With the presence of water and green grass and the references to reclining and eating, there are a number of similarities between the scene in which Jesus multiplies bread and Psalm 23. Reread Mark 6:30–42 aloud. Pause for silent reflection. Then pray Psalm 23 together. End with an Our Father.

♦ Reread Mark 6:45–51 and pray Psalm 46, which has points of similarity with the scene of Jesus on the lake during the storm.

A Living Tradition

Early Morning and Late Night Prayers

This section is a supplement for individual reading.

Jesus prayed before dawn and sometimes in the middle of the night. Here is a prayer for early morning by St. Macarius, a leader of the early monastic movement in Egypt.

Awakening from sleep, I hasten to you, O Master and lover of mankind. As I, through your mercy, begin to fulfill my duties to you, I beseech you to aid me every minute and in every deed. Save me from every earthly evil and from the snare of the Evil One. Save me and lead me to your eternal kingdom. You are my creator and the giver of every blessing. In you I trust and to you I give praise, now and ever and forever. Amen.

Here is a reflection on praying late at night by Blessed Charles de Foucauld, a Frenchman who died in 1916.

Our Lord prayed alone and during the night. . . . Following his example, we should love to pray at night and alone, cherishing such prayer and making a practice of it. We all find it pleasant to be alone with one we love in the midst of silence, when all the world is asleep and darkness covers the earth. How much more pleasant it is, then, to go and spend these hours alone with God. They are hours of incomparable happiness, the blessed hours that led St. Anthony to find the night all too short. Then are the hours when, while everything is silent and asleep, while everything is in darkness, I live at the feet of my God, pouring out my heart in love of him, telling him I love him, while he tells me I shall never love him as much as he loves me, however great my love may be. . . . O my Lord and my God, let me realize as fully as I should the value of such moments! Make me "delight in the Lord" (Psalm 37:4).

A MAN OF THE PEOPLE

Questions to Begin

15 minutes
Use a question or two to get warmed up for the reading.

1 What was the most important rule in your home when you were growing up? Or, if you're a parent, what is the most important rule that you have for your children?

2 Do you now live in the town where you grew up? If not, what is your hometown? Do you return there often? Would you like to live there again?

Opening the Bible

5 minutes
Read the passage aloud. Let individuals take turns reading
paragraphs.

The Background

The Son of the Father became the son of Mary of Nazareth. Jesus lived
in first-century Palestine, spoke Aramaic, the language of Galilee, and
dressed, ate, and worked as people did in his time and place. While
he experienced a unique union with God, he also used the common
prayers that ordinary people in his society used for speaking to God.
He not only prayed in solitude; he also prayed alongside his fellow Jews
in the temple and the synagogue. In our readings this week, we catch
sight of three aspects of Jesus' prayer as a Jewish man of his time. In
our first reading, Jesus quotes a statement from Scripture that was the
centerpiece of Jewish daily prayers. Our second reading shows Jesus
giving thanks at the beginning of a meal as a Jewish host at table.
Finally, we see him taking part in worship in the synagogue in Nazareth,
the small town where he grew up.

The Reading: Mark 12:28–34; Matthew 14:19–21; Luke 4:16–30

Daily Prayer

Mark 12:28 One of the scribes . . . asked him, "Which commandment
is the first of all?" 29 Jesus answered, "The first is, 'Hear, O Israel: the
Lord our God, the Lord is one; 30 you shall love the Lord your God
with all your heart, and with all your soul, and with all your mind,
and with all your strength.' 31 The second is this, 'You shall love your
neighbor as yourself.' There is no other commandment greater than
these." 32 Then the scribe said . . . , "You are right, Teacher; you have
truly said that 'he is one, and besides him there is no other'; 33 and
'to love him with all the heart, and with all the understanding, and
with all the strength,' and 'to love one's neighbor as oneself,'—this is
much more important than all whole burnt offerings and sacrifices."
34 When Jesus saw that he answered wisely, he said to him, "You are
not far from the kingdom of God."

Prayer at Meals

Matthew 14:19 Then he ordered the crowds to sit down on the grass.
Taking the five loaves and the two fish, he looked up to heaven, and

35

blessed and broke the loaves, and gave them to the disciples, and the disciples gave them to the crowds. 20 And all ate and were filled; and they took up what was left over of the broken pieces, twelve baskets full. 21 And those who ate were about five thousand men, besides women and children.

Prayer in the Synagogue

Luke 4:16 When he came to Nazareth, where he had been brought up, he went to the synagogue on the sabbath day, as was his custom. He stood up to read, 17 and the scroll of the prophet Isaiah was given to him. He unrolled the scroll and found the place where it was written:

18 "The Spirit of the Lord is upon me,
because he has anointed me
to bring good news to the poor.
He has sent me to proclaim release to the captives
and recovery of sight to the blind,
to let the oppressed go free,
19 to proclaim the year of the Lord's favor."

20 And he rolled up the scroll, gave it back to the attendant, and sat down. The eyes of all in the synagogue were fixed on him. 21 Then he began to say to them, "Today this scripture has been fulfilled in your hearing." 22 All spoke well of him and were amazed at the gracious words that came from his mouth. They said, "Is not this Joseph's son?" 23 He said to them, "Doubtless you will quote to me this proverb, 'Doctor, cure yourself!' And you will say, 'Do here also in your hometown the things that we have heard you did at Capernaum.'" 24 And he said, "Truly I tell you, no prophet is accepted in the prophet's hometown. 25 But the truth is, there were many widows in Israel in the time of Elijah, when the heaven was shut up three years and six months, and there was a severe famine over all the land; 26 yet Elijah was sent to none of them except to a widow at Zarephath in Sidon. 27 There were also many lepers in Israel in the time of the prophet Elisha, and none of them was cleansed except Naaman the Syrian."

28 When they heard this, all in the synagogue were filled with rage. 29 They got up, drove him out of the town, and led him to the brow of the hill on which their town was built, so that they might hurl him off the cliff. 30 But he passed through the midst of them and went on his way.

10 minutes
Choose questions according to your interest and time.

1 Does the scribe in Mark 12:28 ask Jesus a question because he wants to try to start an argument with him or because he wants to learn from him? Try to base your answer on something in the reading.

2 What invitation is implied in Jesus' words to the scribe in Mark 12:34? What explanation would you offer for the fact that Mark does not tell us how the scribe responded?

3 In Luke 4:23, Jesus thinks that the people of Nazareth will expect him to do in their town what he has done in Capernaum. What has he done in Capernaum? (See our first reading in Week 2.)

4 Is Jesus going to fulfill their expectation? Why?

5 Reread Luke 4:24. If Jesus knew this, why did he go back to Nazareth to preach there?

A Guide to the Reading

If participants have not read this section already, read it aloud. Otherwise go on to "Questions for Application."

Mark 12:28–34. To answer the scribe's question, Jesus quotes the Old Testament book of Deuteronomy (Deuteronomy 6:4–5). For Jews, this was—and still is—one of the best-known passages in the Bible, since every man, and possibly also many women, recited it individually every morning and evening as an expression of faith in God. For Jesus, for the scribe, and for everyone standing around listening to their conversation, the "Hear, O Israel . . ." prayer would be as familiar as the Lord's Prayer is to Christians.

"Hear, O Israel: the Lord our God, the Lord is one." By quoting this text, Jesus affirms that God is the Lord of all, the center of reality, the source of everything. As God's creatures, we owe him the total commitment of our whole being. By adding immediately, "You shall love your neighbor as yourself" (a quotation from Leviticus 19:18), Jesus points us toward the means God gives us for expressing our love for him.

As Jesus prayed "Hear, O Israel . . ." day after day, he must often have pondered the connection between loving his Father and loving the people his Father had given him to care for. As he was growing up, his closest neighbors would have been the people of Nazareth, those whom he returns to speak to in our third reading.

Matthew 14:19–21. We have already read Mark's version of this incident in Jesus' ministry (Week 2). As we now read a small portion of Matthew's version, we focus on a point we passed over last week. Before Jesus multiplies the bread, he gets the people to sit down in an orderly way, so that they can eat like a family having a meal together, rather than like a flock of goats scattered on the hillside. Then, like the head of a household sitting at table at the beginning of a meal, Jesus thanks God for the food. The prayer he offers is probably the customary one for the beginning of a meal.

Thus Jesus does what he saw Joseph doing at home in Nazareth. At the beginning of the meal, Joseph, as head of the house, would hold bread in his hands and say a blessing—probably something like this: "Blessed are you, Lord our God, king of the universe, who brings forth bread from the earth." Then he would break off a piece of the bread and eat it himself and distribute the rest to the others at the table.

As we read in our translation (the New Revised Standard Version), Jesus "looked up to heaven, and blessed and broke the loaves, and gave them to the disciples." This leaves it unclear whether Jesus blessed God or the bread. The Greek text could be translated more literally "Looking up to heaven, he blessed, and having broken, he gave the loaves to his disciples." This more literal translation makes it clearer that Jesus blesses *God*. The prayer he used was this or close to it: "*Blessed are you*, Lord our God, king of the universe, who brings forth bread from the earth."

When God blesses us, he gives us life and provides us with everything we need to sustain our lives. When we bless God, we acknowledge God as the source of every blessing: all fertility, life, and nourishment comes from him.

On the night before he dies, as he eats his final meal with his disciples, Jesus will pray the prayers of thanksgiving in the ritual for Passover—prayers that bless God, acknowledging him as the source of all life and blessing. Then Jesus will go out to demonstrate his confidence that his Father truly *is* the giver of life: he will surrender his life to him on the cross, trusting that his Father will raise him from death. By opening his arms on the cross, Jesus will affirm the faith in the life-giving God that he learned as a child sitting at table with Joseph and Mary. His acceptance of death will be the ultimate human blessing of God—the ultimate declaration that God is the giver of life.

Luke 4:16–30. We have already seen Jesus in the synagogue at Capernaum (Mark 1:21). Week by week, throughout his life, Jesus prayed in the synagogue on the Sabbath—first in Nazareth, where he grew up, and then in other towns in Galilee (Matthew 13:54–58; Mark 1:39; 3:1–6; 6:1–6). This pattern of weekly prayer with his relatives, neighbors, and other fellow Jews was a basic part of his life.

As a trusted, regular participant in the community's weekly Scripture reading and prayer in the synagogue, Jesus can ask the attendant to give him the scroll with the biblical text that he wishes to read (Luke 4:17). He then explains the text to his townspeople. He declares that the prophecy of God's rescuing and saving the poor and needy is beginning to be fulfilled—in him, today! The moment of God's time of liberation and healing has arrived.

The people of Nazareth seem pleased by Jesus' announcement: "All spoke well of him and were amazed at the gracious words that came from his mouth" (Luke 4:22; this seems in contrast to their reaction portrayed in Matthew 13:54–58 and Mark 6:1–6). They welcome Jesus' message about his role in God's plans. How wonderful that a hometown boy has been chosen for this momentous task! They assume that they will be the first to benefit. Jesus will give them priority, won't he? Jesus knows that this is what they will expect: "You will tell me, Physician, heal thyself." In other words, *Prophet, use your power for your own townspeople.*

The people of Nazareth are a microcosm of the Jewish people of the time. Many of them, at least, expect that as members of God's chosen people, they will be the principal beneficiaries—or even the sole beneficiaries—when God brings his judgment and his kingdom into the world. They hope that God will act on their behalf and against their enemies and, in general, against non-Jews, who disregard God and his law.

Jesus bluntly disappoints this expectation. He has not come especially for the in group; he has come for everyone. To make the point, he cites instances in which God acted through Jewish prophets for the good of non-Jews (4:25–27). In God's eyes, there are many "poor . . . captives . . . blind" and "oppressed" people in the world (Luke 4:18), and he intends to help all of them, not just those who belong to the Jewish people. God feels "favor" (Luke 4:19) not only toward Jews but toward all men and women.

Jesus' townspeople are not pleased by this declaration of God's love for the whole world. They are unwilling to open their hearts to share in God's love for outsiders. Jesus' proclamation of the breadth of God's love angers them. They reject him—as he has just predicted they would. A true prophet, he has told them, will be rejected because he preaches an unwelcome message: God's grace to foreigners, outcasts, and enemies. This is not an easy message to accept, particularly because of its practical implication: if you receive the love of the God who loves all, you must share his love with all (see Luke 6:32–36).

Jesus' words in the Nazareth synagogue give us an insight into his prayer. Growing up, as he sat in the synagogue on the Sabbath week after week, he must have reflected on the expansiveness of God's love, which embraces not only the people of Nazareth or of Israel but the whole human race.

Scholars cannot say with certainty what prayers were used in Galilean synagogues in the early first century. But they assume that some later Jewish prayers reflect the usage in the time of Jesus. One prayer that was probably already in use in Jesus' day, which Jews continue to pray in the original Aramaic, begins with these words: "Glorified and sanctified be God's great name throughout the world which he has created according to his will. May he establish his kingdom in your lifetime and during your days, and within the life of the entire house of Israel, speedily and soon." If this prayer was prayed in Nazareth, we may picture Jesus uttering it as an expression of his desire to see God glorified by the coming of his reign in men's and women's lives. Jesus' speech in the synagogue, recorded in Luke 4, suggests that he would have given special emphasis to the prayer's opening words: "Glorified and sanctified be God's great name *throughout the world*."

In every case in our readings this week, we see that there was an inclusive tendency in Jesus' prayer. He took the forms of prayer of his people and prayed them with total love for other people and total commitment to his Father: to love of God he joined love of neighbor; in giving thanks to God, he gave himself; and in seeking the coming of God's reign on earth, he welcomed God's love for the whole human race.

Questions for Application

40 minutes
Choose questions according to your interest and time.

1 What is your pattern of daily prayer? Does it help you to center your life on God each day? How could you grow in spending time with God in daily prayer?

2 What relationship is there between coming closer to God in prayer and growing in love for other people?

3 Do you begin meals and other activities with a prayer of thanks to God? How could you grow in expressing thanks to God for his blessings?

4 In what ways do you tend to limit the circle of your love and concern for other people? Where could you do something to enlarge the circle a bit? Who would you include?

5 In your life, what is the balance between individual prayer and prayer with others?

6 How do this week's readings give you a deeper understanding of Jesus?

7 What encouragement or guidance for your own prayer do you find in Jesus' prayer in this week's readings? How will you respond?

Approach to Prayer

15 minutes
Use this approach—or create your own!

♦ Reread Mark 12:29–31. Pause
for silent reflection. Then close
with this prayer of the late Pope
John Paul II.

Our Lord and our God, through
your resurrection, the love with
which you laid down your life
on the cross became the love that
rolls away the heavy stone that
entombs our hardened hearts.
Help us to love each other with
your undying love. Let us enter
fully into your love for us, as
you entered our humanity to
lead us by the hand on the
path of eternal love. Help us to
die to our selfish ways, as you
put selfishness to death on the
cross. May our lives be a perfect
offering of love to you and to
one another.

Saints in the Making

A Young Woman Discovers Her Calling

This section is a supplement for individual reading.

Here is an excerpt from the autobiography of St. Thérèse of Lisieux (1873–97). Thérèse is speaking to God about her experience of finding her place in the mission of the Church.

I would travel to every land to preach your name, my Beloved, and raise on pagan soil the glorious standard of your cross. One mission alone would not satisfy my longings. I would spread the gospel to the ends of the earth. . . . I would be a missionary, not for a few years only, but, were it possible, from the beginning of the world till the consummation of time. . . .

To such folly as this, what answer will you make? Is there on the face of this earth a soul more feeble than mine? . . .

These aspirations becoming a true martyrdom, I opened, one day, the epistles of St. Paul to seek relief in my sufferings. My eyes fell on the 12th and 13th chapters of the First Epistle to the Corinthians. I read that all cannot become apostles, prophets, and teachers; that the Church is composed of different members; that the eye cannot also be the hand. The answer was clear, but it did not fulfill my desires, or give to me the peace I sought. . . . Without being discouraged I read on, and found comfort. . . . The apostle explains how all perfect gifts are nothing without love, that charity is the most excellent way of going surely to God. At last I had found rest. . . .

Charity provided me with the key to my vocation. I understood that since the Church is a body composed of different members, the noblest and most important of all the organs would not be lacking. I knew that the Church has a heart, that this heart burns with love, and that it is love alone which gives life to its members. . . . I understood that love embraces all vocations, that it is all things, and that it reaches out through all the ages, and to the uttermost limits of the earth. . . .

Beside myself with joy, I cried out: "O Jesus, my Love, at last I have found my vocation. My vocation is love! Yes, I have found my place in the bosom of the Church, and this place, my God, you yourself have given to me: in the heart of the Church . . . I will be *love*!"

Between Discussions

Joy in the Spirit

In the middle of his public life, Jesus sent a large number of his disciples out to towns that he was planning to visit. The disciples were to prepare his way by telling people, "The kingdom of God has come near to you" (Luke 10:1–12). After a while, the disciples returned and gave Jesus a report on their activities. As Luke recounts:

10:17 The seventy returned with joy, saying, "Lord, in your name even the demons submit to us!" 18 He said to them, "I watched Satan fall from heaven like a flash of lightning. 19 See, I have given you authority to tread on snakes and scorpions, and over all the power of the enemy; and nothing will hurt you. 20 Nevertheless, do not rejoice at this, that the spirits submit to you, but rejoice that your names are written in heaven."

21 At that same hour Jesus rejoiced in the Holy Spirit and said, "I thank you, Father, Lord of heaven and earth, because you have hidden these things from the wise and the intelligent and have revealed them to infants; yes, Father, for such was your gracious will. 22 All things have been handed over to me by my Father; and no one knows who the Son is except the Father, or who the Father is except the Son and anyone to whom the Son chooses to reveal him."

23 Then turning to the disciples, Jesus said to them privately, "Blessed are the eyes that see what you see! 24 For I tell you that many prophets and kings desired to see what you see, but did not see it, and to hear what you hear, but did not hear it."

There had probably been some dramatic incidents as Jesus' power worked through his disciples to free people from the influence of evil spirits. Understandably, the disciples were excited by their new empowerment. "Lord, in your name even the demons submit to us!"

Jesus stops them short. In symbolic language, he tells them that he is well aware of their spiritual exploits. Their successful confrontations with the powers of evil are signs of Satan's downfall—a downfall that has begun with Jesus' coming and will be completed at the final coming of God's kingdom (for similar symbolic images of the overthrow of Satan, see John 12:31; Romans 16:20; Revelation 12:7–11; 20:1–3, 10). Jesus, however, is not primarily interested in discussing the disciples' newfound power over evil spirits. He senses the danger that they will become preoccupied with their new access to his power. Instead of being delighted that they can drive away demons, they should take delight in the lasting relationship they have with God (Luke 10:20). Jesus wants his disciples to make this joy the center of their lives.

"Rejoice," he tells them. We may wonder how it is possible to tell someone what they should be happy about. Isn't happiness spontaneous? A person might agree with the idea that knowing God is the greatest possible blessing, yet may not feel excited about it. How, then, can a person obey a command to rejoice? Luke gives the clue when he tells us that "Jesus rejoiced in the Holy Spirit." Jesus invites his disciples to share in the Spirit, and it is this Spirit within us that guides us—freely and spontaneously—to experience joy in knowing God's love for us.

Jesus' outburst into prayer at this point (for similar sudden prayers by Jesus, see John 11:41–42; 12:27–28) is the only instance in Scripture in which someone is said to rejoice in the Spirit. Jesus is so overjoyed by the gift his disciples have received from the Father that he cannot contain himself. He just *has* to turn to his Father and express his gratitude.

Jesus' disciples are ordinary men. They do not have a theological education. They do not occupy positions of authority in Judaism. Yet they have come to know God more deeply and directly than anyone else because they have been humble enough to receive God's revelation of himself in Jesus. To them, the Father has revealed the Son (see 10:21), and the Son has revealed the Father (see 10:22). The disciples have been drawn into the mutual knowledge and love between the Father and the Son. This is the cause of Jesus' joy.

Jesus' prayer strikes a perfect balance of intimacy ("Father") and respect ("Lord of heaven and earth"). From his prayer, we can see what is most important to Jesus: men and women coming to know God's love.

TURNING POINTS

Questions to Begin

15 minutes
Use a question or two to get warmed up for the reading.

1 What's the biggest decision you have made in the last month?

2 When have you had trouble staying awake for something important?

What's Happened

This week, our readings show us Jesus relating to his disciples at three decisive moments during his public life. In every case, we see him praying. In our first reading, Jesus makes an important decision, selecting a dozen of his disciples to be especially close to him. After spending some time with these twelve, Jesus draws them into a conversation about his identity and mission—and the radical implications for them (our second reading). He then makes an extraordinary revelation of himself to his three closest followers (our third reading). Soon after this, he will bring his ministry in Galilee to a close and set out for Jerusalem to face his destiny (Luke 9:51).

The Reading: Luke 6:12–16; 9:18–24, 28–36

Choosing Twelve

6:12 Now during those days he went out to the mountain to pray; and he spent the night in prayer to God. 13 And when day came, he called his disciples and chose twelve of them, whom he also named apostles: 14 Simon, whom he named Peter, and his brother Andrew, and James, and John, and Philip, and Bartholomew, 15 and Matthew, and Thomas, and James son of Alphaeus, and Simon, who was called the Zealot, 16 and Judas son of James, and Judas Iscariot, who became a traitor.

Posing a Crucial Question

9:18 Once when Jesus was praying alone, with only the disciples near him, he asked them, "Who do the crowds say that I am?" 19 They answered, "John the Baptist; but others, Elijah; and still others, that one of the ancient prophets has arisen." 20 He said to them, "But who do you say that I am?" Peter answered, "The Messiah of God."
    21 He sternly ordered and commanded them not to tell anyone, 22 saying, "The Son of Man must undergo great suffering, and be

rejected by the elders, chief priests, and scribes, and be killed, and on the third day be raised."

23 Then he said to them all, "If any want to become my followers, let them deny themselves and take up their cross daily and follow me. 24 For those who want to save their life will lose it, and those who lose their life for my sake will save it."

Revealing His Glory

28 Now about eight days after these sayings Jesus took with him Peter and John and James, and went up on the mountain to pray. 29 And while he was praying, the appearance of his face changed, and his clothes became dazzling white. 30 Suddenly they saw two men, Moses and Elijah, talking to him. 31 They appeared in glory and were speaking of his departure, which he was about to accomplish at Jerusalem.

32 Now Peter and his companions were weighed down with sleep; but since they had stayed awake, they saw his glory and the two men who stood with him. 33 Just as they were leaving him, Peter said to Jesus, "Master, it is good for us to be here; let us make three dwellings, one for you, one for Moses, and one for Elijah"—not knowing what he said. 34 While he was saying this, a cloud came and overshadowed them; and they were terrified as they entered the cloud. 35 Then from the cloud came a voice that said, "This is my Son, my Chosen; listen to him!" 36 When the voice had spoken, Jesus was found alone.

10 minutes
Choose questions according to your interest and time.

1 Luke 9:18 reads: "Once when Jesus was praying alone, with only the disciples near him . . ." How do you picture this scene? (Obviously, there is no one correct answer.)

2 Reread Luke 9:18–22. Does it seem that, before this conversation, Jesus had been publicly declaring himself to be the Messiah?

3 What are the similarities and differences between the statement in Luke 9:35 and that in Luke 3:22 (Week 1)?

4 From the references to Peter in these three readings, what would you conclude about his relationship to Jesus? to the other disciples?

A Guide to the Reading

If participants have not read this section already, read it aloud.
Otherwise go on to "Questions for Application."

6:12–16. Luke shows us Jesus at prayer but does not tell us what he is praying about. It is natural, however, to suppose that Jesus focuses his night of prayer on the action he is to take the following day: selecting, from among the larger group of his disciples (see 10:1), twelve to play a key role in his mission.

This move is especially important for Jesus because it expresses the breathtaking scope of his plans. The people of Israel historically consisted of twelve tribes. By choosing an inner group of twelve disciples, Jesus signals that his mission goes far beyond merely offering some teaching about God; he has come to restore the whole people of Israel—on the basis of personal discipleship to himself.

We can well understand that Jesus would seek wisdom from his Father before filling the twelve openings. These twelve men are going to be the leaders of his movement. Called "apostles"—the Greek word means "those sent"—they will carry his invitation to belong to the renewed people of God to men and women all over the world (Acts 1:8). The availability to people in all succeeding ages of the fruits of Jesus' death and resurrection will depend on the faithfulness of these twelve men.

Does Jesus choose well? If we consider that he is the Son of God, we can only conclude that he makes the perfect choice. If we consider the twelve men, however, we may wonder. None of them possesses wealth or social influence, none is well educated or widely traveled. More important, the Gospels show them to be obtuse and even resistant to Jesus' teaching. When it becomes dangerous to be known as his disciples, the spokesman of the group, Peter, will deny having any relationship with Jesus. The rest of the apostles will simply run away from Jesus—except for Judas, who will betray him to those who want to kill him. It is hard to believe that, from the pool of candidates available to him, Jesus could not have found some more mature and less cowardly trainees for leadership of his movement.

If we think that prayer is a means for finding the best path to success, we would have to ask whether Jesus' prayer before choosing the twelve was effective. But Jesus' idea of success and how to achieve it is different from ours. As he prays here, he is in touch with a deeper wisdom. He discerns a plan in which a loving God works with flawed human beings, patiently bearing with their weaknesses and failings in order to lead them to a place where they become capable of making a contribution to his plans.

9:18–24. A second time, Luke shows us Jesus praying before an important interaction with his disciples. Jesus has an important question to put to the them. Perhaps he prays that they will be prepared to give the correct answer—and to grasp its implications.

Who do the disciples think Jesus is? The crowds of people who flock to his teaching and seek his healing power regard him as a prophet—a spokesperson for God. What do the disciples think? Is he a prophet—or something more?

Peter gives the right answer (9:20). Jesus is the Messiah—the agent of God's end-times action in the world, through whom God will establish his reign over the human race. Like the kings of Israel, this agent will be designated for his task by anointing—smearing with oil (the Hebrew word for anointing gives us the English word *Messiah*; the Greek word for anointing gives us *Christ*). Jesus has been anointed for his task not literally with oil but with the Holy Spirit (3:21–22).

Peter's answer is correct. But neither he nor the other disciples understand its full meaning. They do not grasp what kind of Messiah Jesus is. They assume that he will liberate the people of Israel by military and political means and lead them into a golden age of earthly harmony and blessing (see Acts 1:6).

In response to Peter, Jesus applies a title to himself that his disciples may find puzzling: he refers to himself as "the Son of Man" (9:22). Jews of this time did not use "the Son of Man" as a title for the Messiah. The apostles could find a clue to the meaning of the title in the Old Testament book of Daniel, where a figure called the Son of Man is associated with God's vindication of those who obey him (Daniel 7:13; the NRSV renders the phrase "one like a human being"). Yet Jesus now predicts that, rather than bringing vindication to the obedient and judgment on the rebellious, he, the Son of Man, will fall *under* the power of those who reject God and will be crushed by them! The disciples must be confused—and appalled (compare Mark 8:31–33).

Jesus knows that God's plan for the world involves his suffering and death, and he is ready to give himself wholly to it. He is willing to deny himself and devote himself to God's purposes. And he calls his disciples to do no less (9:23). To "deny" here means to renounce or disown. A person who denies herself says to herself, "Self, I renounce you. You will no longer be my master. I will have a new master now, Jesus Christ." The Greek text indicates that Jesus expects us to "deny" ourselves once and for all but also to renew our denial "daily" (9:23).

By taking up his cross, laying down his life, and rising to new life in God's kingdom, Jesus will become the pioneer on this path of denying self. By following him into God's kingdom, we can "save" the life that we "lose" in the present world (9:24).

Before Jesus initiated the conversation, he was in prayer. I suspect that he was praying for more than guidance as to the right moment to put his question to his disciples. It seems likely that he was pondering the suffering that lay ahead of him on the road of obedience to his Father and the suffering that lay ahead for his disciples—and was asking his Father to give all of us the grace we need to walk behind him on that difficult road.

9:28–36. Jesus spent a night in prayer before choosing the Twelve (6:12). Perhaps here too he is praying at night: notice that the disciples are "weighed down with sleep" (9:32).

In any case, "while he was praying, the appearance of his face changed" (9:29). By telling us twice that Jesus was praying (9:28–29), Luke underlines the connection between Jesus' prayer and the change in his appearance. In Scripture, prayer is sometimes described as seeking to be face-to-face with God (see Psalm 27:8–9), and God is sometimes said to let his face shine on those who seek his blessing (Numbers 6:25; Psalm 67:1; 80:3, 7). Moses communicated so directly with God that, after he prayed, his face would glow from the divine radiance that had been shining on him (Exodus 34:29–35). Here, Jesus' face is radiant because he too is face to face with God—in an utterly unique way (John 1:18; 6:46). Moses' face *reflected* God's glory; the radiance on Jesus' face shines from within. The divine glory belongs to Jesus as God's Son.

But the sudden visibility of Jesus' glory at this particular moment seems due to something going on between Jesus and the Father as Jesus prays. A clue to the content of Jesus' communication with his Father here lies in the timing of this event. Jesus' mountaintop prayer occurs a few days after he has spoken to his disciples about his approaching death and shortly before he begins the journey to Jerusalem that will end at the cross. His prayer, then, probably has something to do with his imminent death and resurrection. Confirmation of this connection lies in the conversation he has with Moses and Elijah, who appear beside him. They are talking with him about the "departure" he is about to make in Jerusalem (9:31)—a departure for which Luke uses the Greek word for "exodus." In this way, Luke links Jesus' departure from this world to the Israelites' exodus, or departure, from Egypt. Just as Moses led the Israelites out of slavery by their exodus, or departure, from Egypt, so Jesus will bring men and women on an exodus from sin, guilt, and death by his departure from earthly life through death and resurrection. Thus it seems that in his prayer here, Jesus meditates on this gift of himself that he is about to make to his Father and on the life that will flow from his offering for all humanity. As he contemplates these events, he is deeply moved and radiates an unimaginable light.

The disciples grasp little of what is going on (9:33). But the vision undoubtedly gives them much food for thought. They carry down from the mountain the memory of their master in prayer and of the Father's words to them: "This is my Son, my Chosen; listen to him!"

Questions for Application

40 minutes
Choose questions according to your interest and time.

1 When have you prayed before making a decision? In what way did you experience God's guidance?

2 Have you ever prayed before an important conversation—with a friend, family member, someone at work? What was the result?

3 Often, as in Luke 9:20, Jesus asks his disciples questions, rather than simply making statements to them. Have you found that it is sometimes more effective to ask a question than make a statement?

4 When have you found that there can be more joy in giving than in receiving?

5 Have you ever had an experience of God's glory in prayer—in private prayer, in the liturgy, in other forms of prayer? If so, how has this affected your relationship with God?

6 In prayer, do you listen to Jesus as the disciples were challenged to do at the Transfiguration?

7 How do this week's readings give you a deeper understanding of Jesus?

8 What encouragement or guidance for your own prayer do you find in Jesus' prayer in this week's readings? How will you respond?

Approach to Prayer

15 minutes
Use this approach—or create your own!

♦ Pray Psalm 27 together as a
prayer for God's guidance in any
decisions that the participants
face. Pause for silent reflection.
End together with an Our Father.

Saints in the Making

Now Hear This

This section is a supplement for individual reading.

B y his night prayer, Jesus left us an example of seeking God before major decisions. For centuries, Catholics have used a "novena" as a way of seeking to learn God's will. The word comes from the Latin for "nine." It refers to the practice of praying for a particular purpose every day for nine days. The practice is modeled on the prayer of Jesus' first disciples, who prayed together for nine days from his ascension into heaven to the coming of the Holy Spirit at Pentecost (see Acts 1:4–14; 2:1–4). Catholics use novenas not only to pray for guidance but also to pray for any need—spiritual or material.

There is no one formula for praying a novena. Probably hundreds of novena prayers have been composed and circulated. Some seek the intercession of Mary or another saint. Some are addressed directly to God. There is nothing magical about any of these novena prayers. All prayer relies on God's love and power. Thus anyone can use any prayer they wish for a novena.

My own life has been greatly affected by a novena. During World War II, a Navy officer named Roger Bourassa struggled to know God's path for his life. He was trying to decide whether—when the war was over—he should try to get married or enter a monastery. Faced with such a momentous decision, he decided to make a *triple* novena—twenty-seven days of prayer to the Blessed Mother—to seek God's guidance. As it happened, on the last day of his prayer, a fellow officer set him up with a blind date. If ever there was an answer to a young man's prayer, it was Roma Richard. Roger and Roma hit it off immediately. They got married just as the war was ending. Soon their first daughter, Louise, arrived in the world.

Ever since Louise and I got married, I have thanked God that my father-in-law prayed his novena—and that God answered it so well.

NOT MY WILL BUT YOURS

Questions to Begin

15 minutes
Use a question or two to get warmed up for the reading.

---

1 In what recent situation might someone have said to you, "I told you so"? Did they say it?

---

2 If a friend of yours needed you and knew you were with friends, in what place would he or she go looking for you?

5 minutes
Read the passage aloud. Let individuals take turns reading paragraphs.

What's Happened

The scene is Jerusalem. It is the night before Jesus' death. He has just finished his Last Supper with his disciples.

The Reading: Mark 14:26–50

A Painful Conversation

26 When they had sung the hymn, they went out to the Mount of Olives.

27 And Jesus said to them, "You will all become deserters; for it is written,

'I will strike the shepherd,
and the sheep will be scattered.'

28 But after I am raised up, I will go before you to Galilee."

29 Peter said to him, "Even though all become deserters, I will not."

30 Jesus said to him, "Truly I tell you, this day, this very night, before the cock crows twice, you will deny me three times."

31 But he said vehemently, "Even though I must die with you, I will not deny you." And all of them said the same.

Anguished Prayer

32 They went to a place called Gethsemane; and he said to his disciples, "Sit here while I pray." 33 He took with him Peter and James and John, and began to be distressed and agitated. 34 And he said to them, "I am deeply grieved, even to death; remain here, and keep awake."

35 And going a little farther, he threw himself on the ground and prayed that, if it were possible, the hour might pass from him. 36 He said, "Abba, Father, for you all things are possible; remove this cup from me; yet, not what I want, but what you want."

37 He came and found them sleeping; and he said to Peter, "Simon, are you asleep? Could you not keep awake one hour?

^{38} Keep awake and pray that you may not come into the time of trial; the spirit indeed is willing, but the flesh is weak."

^{39} And again he went away and prayed, saying the same words. ^{40} And once more he came and found them sleeping, for their eyes were very heavy; and they did not know what to say to him. ^{41} He came a third time and said to them, "Are you still sleeping and taking your rest? Enough! The hour has come; the Son of Man is betrayed into the hands of sinners. ^{42} Get up, let us be going. See, my betrayer is at hand."

Betrayal and Abandonment

^{43} Immediately, while he was still speaking, Judas, one of the twelve, arrived; and with him there was a crowd with swords and clubs, from the chief priests, the scribes, and the elders. ^{44} Now the betrayer had given them a sign, saying, "The one I will kiss is the man; arrest him and lead him away under guard." ^{45} So when he came, he went up to him at once and said, "Rabbi!" and kissed him. ^{46} Then they laid hands on him and arrested him.

^{47} But one of those who stood near drew his sword and struck the slave of the high priest, cutting off his ear. ^{48} Then Jesus said to them, "Have you come out with swords and clubs to arrest me as though I were a bandit? ^{49} Day after day I was with you in the temple teaching, and you did not arrest me. But let the scriptures be fulfilled."

^{50} All of them deserted him and fled.

10 minutes
Choose questions according to your interest and time.

1 Suppose you had been one of the disciples that night, walking with Jesus to Gethsemane. What would *you* have said to him in response to his saying, "You will all become deserters" (14:27)?

2 What poor choices did the disciples make that night, in each of the three scenes in this reading? What better choices might they have made? Why didn't they make better choices?

3 Consider how the disciples relate to Jesus in Mark 1:37–38; 6:35–37, 49–50 (Week 2), in Luke 9:20, 33 (Week 4), and in our reading this week. How well do the disciples grasp who Jesus is and what he is doing? Are they generally on the same page with their master?

4 How would you describe Jesus' attitude toward his disciples in this reading?

5 Based simply on this reading, what kind of man does Jesus seem to be?

A Guide to the Reading

*If participants have not read this section already, read it aloud.
Otherwise go on to "Questions for Application."*

14:26–31. After the Passover meal, Jesus walks with his disciples
from the home where they have eaten, out of Jerusalem, and down
into the Kidron Valley, east of the city. If the disciples are feeling
mellow after the meal, Jesus shatters their mood with harsh
realism. "You will all become deserters," he declares. He wants
them to know that he foresees that they will abandon him—and
that afterward he will be willing to be reconciled with them: "After
I am raised up, I will go before you to Galilee." He does not want
their remorse for abandoning him to bring them to despair (contrast
Judas in Matthew 27:3–5). But the disciples do not recognize Jesus'
pastoral purpose. Rejecting his assurance of future reconciliation,
they insist that they will never abandon him.

As Jesus' disciples cluster around him, vehemently
declaring their faithfulness, he seems strangely alone. The men
around him do not understand him or themselves or the events that
are about to take place.

14:32. On the hill on the other side of the Kidron Valley,
the group reaches a grove of olive trees called Gethsemane, a
place where Jesus has often spent time with his disciples. He
stops here, even though Judas knows it is a likely place to find him
(John 18:1–2). It almost seems as though Jesus is arriving for a
prearranged meeting.

14:33–34. Why does Jesus keep Peter, James, and John
close to him while he prays? Is it for companionship? Perhaps.
Before this, however, Jesus has never looked to his disciples for
encouragement or consolation. They have often seemed to be in a
fog of incomprehension or misunderstanding about him, failing to
grasp his plans even after repeated explanations (6:52; 8:17–21,
31–33; 9:30–32; 10:32). What support could they offer him now, as
he enters his mysterious mission's most difficult phase?

14:35. After getting Peter, James, and John settled, Jesus
goes only "a little farther" to pray. Presumably, he prays aloud, as
people in this culture usually do, even when praying alone.

In terrible aloneness, Jesus prays—and, quite possibly,
keeps watch. From Gethsemane, there is a clear view of Jerusalem.
The temple lies directly across the Kidron Valley. A group of people

coming out of the temple gate and crossing the valley would be easily visible under the full moon of Passover. As Jesus cries out to his Father in the garden, he may be keeping an eye out for his betrayer's approach.

Jesus could get away from Judas and the arresting party by taking the path up the dark Mount of Olives. The Judean wilderness begins on the other side of the hill. It would be easy to escape the pursuers there. At the beginning of his public life, however, Jesus refused the Devil's suggestion to feed himself by miraculously turning a stone into bread (Luke 4:3–4). Now he refuses to save himself from suffering by running away. He knows that his death lies at the center of God's plan for the human race. So he stays in Gethsemane. Thus, even as Jesus appeals to his Father to change his plans, to find some other way to redeem the human race besides his death, he is already offering himself to the Father by the simple act of remaining in the garden. Jesus' sacrifice of himself has begun.

14:36. This is no easy offering. In Jesus' heart, absolute determination to obey his Father runs up against fear and dread. Only by profound humility and love for his Father can Jesus add to his prayer for deliverance the words of resignation: "Yet, not what I want, but what you want."

The crucial word in Jesus' prayer is the one by which he addresses God: *Abba*. Mark has preserved the Aramaic word, rather than translating it into Greek. *Abba* means "Father," or "Dad." It is the respectful but affectionate form of address that an adult child would use in speaking to his or her father. In a single word, Jesus expresses the unbounded love, affection, and trust that is the basis for his submission to God's plan.

How *can* Jesus plead with his Father to change his plan? It is difficult to probe the mysteries here: the apparent possibility of a divergence of the will of the Son from the will of the Father, and the apparent clash between Jesus' divine will and human will. What is clear, however, is that Jesus, while being totally willing to obey his Father, expresses to his Father with complete frankness his human reluctance to undergo the suffering that lies ahead of him. For

Jesus, prayer was never just a form of right and appropriate words. Prayer was a matter of earnest and honest conversation, a heart-to-heart encounter with God.

14:37–38. "Keep awake and pray" (14:38). With this urgent instruction, Jesus may indicate the reason he has kept the three disciples near him. He wants them to pray. And knowing that they are sleepy, he keeps them close to him, so that he can help them stay awake.

Why is it so important that they pray? Jesus has predicted that the disciples will desert him. But this prediction is not an immutable decree of fate. Nothing will *compel* them to abandon him. Certainly, when the temple police arrive, the disciples will sense danger and be tempted to flee—and they will be too weak to resist the temptation, by their own strength. But God's help could counterbalance their fear. So Jesus urges them to pray. If only they would pray, his prediction might not come to pass. Thus, at the very moment when he feels the greatest need in his entire life to focus on his own inner struggle, Jesus interrupts his own tormented prayer *twice* to check on whether his disciples are praying for themselves. And he does this despite the fact that he foresees that they will not pray and will abandon him. His love for his disciples has never seemed so tender or so profound.

Jesus speaks of "spirit" and "flesh." These are two dimensions of the human person: "spirit" being the total person in terms of mind and will (2:8; 8:12), "flesh" the total person in terms of physical and psychological needs and desires. Jesus' words to his disciples about the willingness of the spirit and the weakness of the flesh come straight from his own experience. One side of him declares to God, "Your will be done," while the other pleads, "Take this suffering away from me!"

The difference between Jesus and his disciples is not that they experience an inner conflict while he does not. Jesus' flesh is as human and frail as theirs; he too feels the terror of death. The difference is that he brings his inner struggle to God; the disciples do not. Peter, James, and John have not faced up to their weakness

(14:26–31). Consequently, they fail to pray. They fall asleep. Soon they will run away.

Jesus tells them, "Pray that you may not come into the time of trial." "Trial" here means temptation to do evil. To "come into" temptation is to yield to it, to agree to it, to give oneself over to it (just as going into the kingdom of heaven means to give oneself over to it, to belong to it, to be taken into it—Matthew 5:20; 7:21; 18:3). Jesus is not telling the disciples to ask God not to be tempted. He knows that temptation is coming their way. He urges them to pray that God would keep them from *going into* temptation—to pray that God would preserve them from falling away into sin.

Jesus himself does not pray in the particular way that he recommends to his disciples. He does not explicitly ask God to give him the strength to withstand temptation. Apparently, Jesus finds God's help by his totally honest and submissive struggle with God in prayer.

14:39–42. Does Jesus hope that the sound of his praying will encourage the three disciples to pray also? Does he intend his prayer to be a model for theirs? If so, he is disappointed, for his prayer has no effect on the disciples. Listening to their master's anguished pleading with God, just yards away, they fall asleep, over and over again. Their abandonment of Jesus has begun.

While the disciples sleep, Jesus prays on, alone. God does not change his plan or give his Son any verbal response. Yet it seems that Jesus finds strength in his anguished pleading with his Father, for he deals decisively with the situation that follows. Seeing the arresting party approaching, Jesus speaks resolutely to his disciples: "Let us be going. See, my betrayer is at hand." These are his last words to his disciples before his death. They show him to be the shepherd to the end: "Let *us* be going." Jesus has not stopped leading his disciples, trying to keep them close to him, or identifying himself with them.

14:43–50. Jesus entered Gethsemane surrounded by disciples claiming to be loyal. He leaves surrounded by police, his disciples nowhere to be seen. Jesus goes to face his destiny abandoned by all except his Father.

Questions for Application

40 minutes
Choose questions according to your interest and time.

1   Have you ever asked others to join you in prayer in a difficult time?

2   When has your prayer resembled Jesus' prayer in Gethsemane? How did God respond to your prayer?

3   When have you discovered your own weakness in trying to obey God? What did you learn from the experience?

4   What kind of balance should there be between using set prayers and speaking directly to God in your own words? When you speak to God in your own words, are you direct and straightforward with him about your thoughts and feelings?

5 What is the role of prayer in helping a person resist temptation?

6 Do you know someone who faces a difficult decision or is suffering? How could you support that person in prayer? How might you pray with them?

7 How do this week's readings give you a deeper understanding of Jesus?

8 What encouragement or guidance for your own prayer do you find in Jesus' prayer in this week's readings? How will you respond?

Approach to Prayer

15 minutes
Use this approach—or create your own!

♦ Pray together Psalm 143 as a plea for God's mercy and as an expression of trust in God. Pause briefly for silent reflection. Close with an Our Father.

Saints in the Making

A Prisoner's Prayer

This section is a supplement for individual reading.

Vietnamese bishop Francis Xavier Nguyen Van Thuan was imprisoned by his country's Communist government from 1975 to 1988. Here are excerpts of the prayer he wrote the day after his arrest.

Jesus . . .
There are so many confused feelings in my head:
Sadness, fear, tension,
My heart is torn to pieces for having been taken away from my
        people. . . .
But in this sea of extreme bitterness
I feel freer than ever before.
I have nothing with me,
Not even a penny,
Nothing but my rosary and the companionship of Jesus and Mary. . . .
In the darkness of this night, in the midst of this ocean of anxiety, of
        nightmares,
I slowly wake up again:
"I must confront reality:
I am in prison.
If I wait for an opportune moment
To do something truly great,
How many times will such occasions actually present themselves?
No, I will seize the occasions that present themselves every day.
I must accomplish ordinary actions in an extraordinary way."
Jesus, I will not wait,
I will live the present moment,
Filling it to the brim with love. . . .
The life of hope is made of brief moments of hope.
As you, Jesus, always did what pleased your Father,
Every minute I want to say:
"Jesus, I love you,
And my life is always 'a new and eternal covenant' with you.
Every minute I want to sing with your Church:
Glory be to the Father, and to the Son, and to the Holy Spirit."

The Darkest Hour

Questions to Begin

15 minutes
Use a question or two to get warmed up for the reading.

1 When have you been glad to have someone stand by you in a difficult situation?

2 If it were up to you, where would you choose to die? Who would you want with you?

Opening the Bible

5 minutes
Read the passage aloud. Let individuals take turns reading paragraphs.

What's Happened

Jesus has been interrogated by the religious and civil leaders in Jerusalem, condemned to death, taken out of the city, and crucified on a rocky knoll near one of the city's gates.

The Reading: Mark 15:25–37; Psalm 22:1–2, 7–11, 14–24

Jesus' Final Prayer

Mark 15:25 It was nine o'clock in the morning when they crucified him. 26 The inscription of the charge against him read, "The King of the Jews." 27 And with him they crucified two bandits, one on his right and one on his left. 29 Those who passed by derided him, shaking their heads and saying, "Aha! You who would destroy the temple and build it in three days, 30 save yourself, and come down from the cross!" 31 In the same way the chief priests, along with the scribes, were also mocking him among themselves and saying, "He saved others; he cannot save himself. 32 Let the Messiah, the King of Israel, come down from the cross now, so that we may see and believe." Those who were crucified with him also taunted him.

33 When it was noon, darkness came over the whole land until three in the afternoon. 34 At three o'clock Jesus cried out with a loud voice, "Eloi, Eloi, lema sabachthani?" which means, "My God, my God, why have you forsaken me?" 35 When some of the bystanders heard it, they said, "Listen, he is calling for Elijah." 36 And someone ran, filled a sponge with sour wine, put it on a stick, and gave it to him to drink, saying, "Wait, let us see whether Elijah will come to take him down." 37 Then Jesus gave a loud cry and breathed his last.

An Anguished Appeal

Psalm 22:1 My God, my God, why have you forsaken me?
    Why are you so far from helping me, from the words
        of my groaning?
  2 O my God, I cry by day, but you do not answer;
    and by night, but find no rest. . . .
  7 All who see me mock at me;
    they make mouths at me, they shake their heads;

73

8 "Commit your cause to the LORD; let him
        deliver—
    let him rescue the one in whom he delights!"
9 Yet it was you who took me from the womb;
    you kept me safe on my mother's breast.
10 On you I was cast from my birth,
        and since my mother bore me you have been my
        God.
11 Do not be far from me,
        for trouble is near
        and there is no one to help. . . .
14 I am poured out like water,
        and all my bones are out of joint;
    my heart is like wax;
        it is melted within my breast;
15 my mouth is dried up like a potsherd,
        and my tongue sticks to my jaws;
        you lay me in the dust of death.
16 For dogs are all around me;
        a company of evildoers encircles me. . . .
17 . . . They stare and gloat over me;
18 they divide my clothes among themselves,
        and for my clothing they cast lots.
19 But you, O LORD, do not be far away!
        O my help, come quickly to my aid!
20 Deliver my soul from the sword,
        my life from the power of the dog!
21   Save me from the mouth of the lion!

    From the horns of the wild oxen you have rescued me.
22 I will tell of your name to my brothers and sisters;
        in the midst of the congregation I will praise you:
23 You who fear the LORD, praise him!
        All you offspring of Jacob, glorify him;
        stand in awe of him, all you offspring of Israel!
24 For he did not despise or abhor
        the affliction of the afflicted;
    he did not hide his face from me,
        but heard when I cried to him.

Questions for Careful Reading

10 minutes
Choose questions according to your interest and time.

1 In Mark's account, how long does Jesus hang on the cross before he dies?

2 Mark tells us that the sky became dark at noon (15:33). What might be the significance of this darkness?

3 From Jesus' dying words (Mark 15:34), what would you conclude about the severity of his suffering?

4 The psalm seems to mingle images of sickness with images of persecution by enemies. Which images seem to reflect sickness? persecution?

5 What does the action of the psalmist's enemies in Psalm 22:18 suggest regarding the likelihood of the psalmist's recovery?

6 What points of similarity between the psalm and Mark's account of Jesus' crucifixion can you find?

A Guide to the Reading

If participants have not read this section already, read it aloud. Otherwise go on to "Questions for Application."

Hanging in torment on a cross set up beside a busy road, Jesus is exposed to the mockery of people passing by. "Save yourself, and come down from the cross!" they shout at him. "He saved others; he cannot save himself" (Mark 15:30–31). In fact, Jesus *could* save himself. But "save yourself," like "serve yourself," has never been his way. Jesus has come to save life (Mark 3:4)—but not his own. He has come into the world to relinquish his life in order to restore our life with God (Mark 10:45). If he saved himself now, he would fail in his mission.

From the cross, Jesus cries out, "My God, my God, why have you forsaken me?" Does he suddenly doubt his Father's love? St. Ambrose, a great fourth-century bishop and theologian, wrote: "It is not his divinity that doubts, but his human soul. As God he was not distressed, but as a human he was capable of being distressed. . . . As human, therefore, he speaks on the cross, bearing with him our terrors. For amid dangers it is a very human response to think ourself abandoned."

Some interpreters regard Jesus' cry from the cross as an expression of absolute despair: he suddenly realizes that his conviction that God will bring the kingdom through his suffering and death has been a total mistake. In his dying moments, these interpreters say, Jesus realizes that he has gone astray from God's plans and that God has now abandoned him to a meaningless death.

It is significant, however, that Jesus' cry is a quotation of the first line of Psalm 22 (Mark cites it in Jesus' native Aramaic). Undoubtedly Jesus knows the psalm well. We may assume that the whole psalm is in his mind as he cries out the opening words, even though, struggling for breath, he is incapable of uttering the entire prayer. Thus, for insight into Jesus' state of mind as he cries out, "My God, my God, why have you forsaken me?" we can look at Psalm 22.

Psalm 22 is the prayer of a person in extreme suffering. The psalmist is undergoing physical torment—the exact nature of it is not clear—and also a kind of social torment, for enemies make fun of the psalmist's condition. In addition, the psalmist feels the pain of abandonment by God. God has failed to protect the psalmist from his or her terrible suffering. The psalmist is appalled by this divine abandonment, which conflicts with the psalmist's previous experience of God as trustworthy and kind (Psalm 22:9–10). So the psalmist assaults God with anguished protest: "Why have you forsaken me?" (Psalm 22:1).

Taken by itself, the psalmist's question—"Why have you forsaken me?"—might sound like an angry challenge to God to explain his neglect of the sufferer. The psalmist, however, is not engaging in a Job-like argument with God. Psalm 22 is not an inquiry into why God allows suffering. It is a cry for help. The psalmist is not trying to get God to explain himself but to pay attention to the psalmist's suffering. The psalmist assumes that the sight of such atrocious pain will move God, who is compassionate, to act. The psalmist's question implicitly reproaches God—*You used to be faithful to me. Where is your faithfulness now?*—to spur God to come to the rescue. After the opening question, the psalmist piles one horrendous image of his suffering on another—every image designed to give weight to the urgent appeal: "You, O Lord, do not be far away! O my help, come quickly to my aid!" (Psalm 22:19).

Then Psalm 22 makes a sudden turn. "From the horns of the wild oxen you have rescued me," the psalmist declares (Psalm 22:21). With this announcement that God *has* come to his or her aid, the psalmist shifts from crying for help to giving thanks. No longer a plea for God's help, the psalm becomes a celebration of God's triumph over the forces that threaten human life. The psalmist declares that he or she has received such tremendous divine help that awestruck men and women everywhere will worship God.

What light does Psalm 22 shed on Jesus as he prays on the cross? By quoting Psalm 22, Jesus expresses his misery at the fact that God has not shielded him from torment and contempt. St. Augustine commented: "Out of the voice of the psalmist, which our Lord transferred to himself, he spoke these words: 'My God, my God, why have you forsaken me?' He is doubtless forsaken in the sense that his plea was not directly granted." Nevertheless, as we have seen, the psalm that Jesus begins is not a cry of despair but an anguished appeal for help.

At both Gethsemane and Golgotha, Jesus expresses the terror and pain that any of us might experience in a similar situation. In Gethsemane, by pleading with God to alter his plan ("Let this cup pass"), Jesus reveals that he is overwhelmed with dread. At Golgotha, he expresses his physical agony and terrible loneliness with the cry of one who feels forsaken by God ("Why have you forsaken me?"). Yet at both moments, Jesus clings to his Father. In Gethsemane, he submits his fear to God by praying, "Not my will but yours be done." On the cross, even in his experience of utter abandonment, he continues to cry out to his Father: "My God, my God." Despite God's apparent absence from the scene of Jesus' suffering, Jesus continues to relate to God as his own.

Thus, on the cross as in the garden, Jesus presents his human experience to God. In the garden, he goes so far as to express his own will in contrast to his Father's. On the cross, he complains to his Father for utterly abandoning him. Yet by the very fact that he continues to express himself to God, his relationship with God remains unbroken. Indeed, nothing more clearly reveals the depth and strength of Jesus' relationship with his Father than these anguished prayers.

Notice that the bystanders at the crucifixion do not interpret Jesus' prayer as a cry of despair. Apparently they do not realize that he is quoting Psalm 22, since, from the similarity of the two words in Aramaic, they confuse the word for God with the name of the prophet Elijah (Mark 15:34–35). Despite their misunderstanding, however, they seem to have correctly grasped that Jesus is calling on God for help. What they do not comprehend is that God will respond to Jesus' prayer not by saving him *from* death but by bringing him *through* death into the triumph of resurrection (Mark 8:31; 9:31; 10:33–34). This triumph will benefit all humanity—just as God's astounding help to the psalmist will have a great effect on people everywhere (Psalm 22:22–31).

Jesus' final prayer certainly lacks any trace of the exultation of the concluding section of Psalm 22. Indeed, no bleaker last words can be imagined than Jesus' praying of Psalm 22:1. Yet the triumphant ending of Psalm 22 communicates the confidence in God's saving action that Jesus earlier expressed when he predicted his death and resurrection to his disciples (Mark 10:45). No matter how far removed from Jesus' experience on the cross, the joyous ending of the psalm expresses the faith and hope that led him there.

But this is hidden from the bystanders. In response to Jesus' prayer, a man "runs" to get Jesus a little wine to drink. Probably the man hurries because he thinks Jesus is about to die and he wants to keep him alive a little longer to see whether Elijah will really appear and rescue him. The man's gesture is not mercy but mockery.

So Jesus dies, abandoned by all, seemingly even by God. He prays as one forsaken by God—and apparently receives no answer. Tortured to death, mocked to the end, his trust in God seems discredited.

In later times, some of Jesus' followers have found themselves in similar situations. Perhaps Mark's first readers were in such a situation. There is reason to think that he wrote his Gospel in Rome for Christians undergoing a terrible persecution by the emperor Nero. In his account of Jesus' death, Mark's message is that the inner reality on Golgotha was different from the outer one. Jesus' radical devotion to God's will, his courage to go on crying out to God even when God seemed silent and absent, and his acceptance of suffering as the means by which God was going to bring his kingdom—all this has released us from the stranglehold of sin and death (Mark 10:45). Mark suggests that by faithful prayer in pain and sorrow, in imitation of Jesus, we can share in the same inner reality. In the midst of God's apparent absence, even on the brink of despair, Jesus' disciples can pray—and, by praying, we can play a part in his bringing the kingdom of God.

Questions for Application

40 minutes
Choose questions according to your interest and time.

1 When do you feel tempted to lose hope? At those times, do you pray? What do you say to God? What is the result?

2 Recall a time of suffering in your life. How did you pray then? What did you learn about God? about prayer? about yourself?

3 What are effective ways of helping a suffering person realize that they are not alone? Consider various situations and kinds of suffering.

4 Who do you know that is suffering now? What could you do to support them?

5 What can you learn for your own prayer from Psalm 22?

6 When Jesus was in pain, he prayed a psalm. What place do the psalms have in your prayer in times of distress? How could you make the psalms more a part of your own prayer?

7 How do this week's readings give you a deeper understanding of Jesus?

8 What encouragement or guidance for your own prayer do you find in Jesus' prayer in this week's readings? How will you respond?

Approach to Prayer

15 minutes
Use this approach—or create your own!

♦ Pause for a moment of silent reflection on people you know who are experiencing suffering or sorrow. Pray the whole of Psalm 22 with these people in mind. End with a Glory to the Father.

Saints in the Making

Eyes on the Cross

This section is a supplement for individual reading.

Jesus died in a state of desolation, crying out to God—who seemed to have hidden himself from him in his final suffering. Yet, through the ages, Christians facing death have found Jesus' death on the cross a great consolation. Many have chosen to die with a crucifix before them or even in their hands. One of these was John XXIII, who was pope from 1958 to 1963. In September 1962, he was diagnosed with stomach cancer. The following May, his doctors informed him that there was no further treatment for his condition. Death seemed imminent. Three days before he died, after receiving the sacrament of anointing of the sick, Pope John sat up in bed and spoke a little with Church officials, medical personnel, and the nuns who had served as his housekeepers. He pointed them toward the crucifix on his wall.

The secret of my ministry is in that crucifix you see opposite my bed. It's there so that I can see it in my first waking moment and before going to sleep. It's there, also, so that I can talk to it during the long evening hours. Look at it, see it as I see it. Those open arms have been the program of my pontificate: they say that Christ died for all, for all. No one is excluded from his love, from his forgiveness. . . .

I had the great grace to be born into a Christian family, modest and poor but with the fear of the Lord. I had the grace to be called by God as a child: I never thought of anything else, I never had any other ambition. . . . Along the way I've met holy priests and good superiors. . . . All helped me and loved me. I had lots of encouragement.

For my part, I'm not aware of having offended anyone, but if I have, I beg their forgiveness; and if you know of anyone who has not been edified by my attitudes or actions, ask them to have compassion on me and to forgive me. In this last hour I feel calm and sure that my Lord, in his mercy, will not reject me.

Pope John died on June 3, 1963. In 2000, Pope John Paul II gave John XXIII the title "Blessed," moving him into the final stage toward recognition as a saint in the Catholic Church.

I Am Asking on Their Behalf

John 17

In John's Gospel, Jesus prays a lengthy prayer at the end of the Last Supper—his longest prayer recorded in any of the Gospels. It is a solemn moment, just before he goes out to submit to a painful death on our behalf, and his prayer is also solemn. Jesus sums up the meaning of his life and death, and offers himself to the Father with an appeal for his disciples in every age. His prayer takes us to the heart of his relationship with his Father. Let's examine it one section at a time.

Jesus begins by praying for himself. Sitting at table with his disciples, he looks up to heaven and says:

1 . . . Father, the hour has come; glorify your Son so that the Son may glorify you, 2 since you have given him authority over all people, to give eternal life to all whom you have given him. 3 And this is eternal life, that they may know you, the only true God, and Jesus Christ whom you have sent. 4 I glorified you on earth by finishing the work that you gave me to do. 5 So now, Father, glorify me in your own presence with the glory that I had in your presence before the world existed.

6 I have made your name known to those whom you gave me from the world. They were yours, and you gave them to me, and they have kept your word. 7 Now they know that everything you have given me is from you; 8 for the words that you gave to me I have given to them, and they have received them and know in truth that I came from you; and they have believed that you sent me.

Jesus declares that he has glorified the Father (17:4) and looks forward to glorifying him again (17:1). *Glorify* is not an everyday English word. What does it mean here? We can grasp Jesus' meaning by comparing his words "I glorified you on earth" (17:4) with his words "I have made your name known" (17:6). The two statements are parallel. Jesus has "glorified" the Father by making known his Father's "name," that is, by making known the Father's true nature and character. During his public life, Jesus has miraculously healed the sick and disabled and supplied food and drink; he even brought someone back from the dead (1:14; 2:11;

11:43–44; 12:28). All these actions have been signs of God's love.
They have revealed God's character. Thus Jesus has "glorified" God:
he has displayed God's love; seeing God's love, people will glorify
God, that is, they will honor him and love him in return.

Now, however, Jesus has finished working such signs.
The moment has come (17:1) to display the reality toward which
the signs pointed. The Father's love for the human race will be
completely revealed in Jesus' offering of himself on the cross.
His death will be the greatest expression of God's love because,
by Jesus' life-giving gift of himself in death, God will cleanse us
of our sins, enabling us to receive his Spirit and to live in hope
of sharing in his life forever (3:16; 20:22–23). Thus by accepting
death on a cross as the Father's will, Jesus will perfectly "glorify"
the Father—he will perfectly reveal the Father's immense love for
the human race.

Jesus asks the Father to glorify him in return (17:5). How
will Jesus be glorified? Since Jesus' glory is the same as the
Father's, his glory, too, consists in love. Jesus will be glorified by
his death because, by accepting this death as part of God's plan
for us, Jesus will show his total love for his Father (14:31) and his
total love for us.

Jesus' meaning here is very dense. By asking the Father
to glorify him, Jesus is also asking that his life, offered to the
Father on the cross, may be an acceptable sacrifice. He is asking
that the Father will raise him from death into heavenly glory. He is
asking that, through his death, the Father will bring his kingdom
into the world.

Jesus moves on to pray for the disciples who are
sitting at table with him.

⁹ I am asking on their behalf; I am not asking on behalf of the world,
but on behalf of those whom you gave me, because they are yours.
¹⁰ All mine are yours, and yours are mine; and I have been glorified
in them. ¹¹ And now I am no longer in the world, but they are in
the world, and I am coming to you. Holy Father, protect them in
your name that you have given me, so that they may be one, as we

are one. ¹² While I was with them, I protected them in your name that you have given me. I guarded them, and not one of them was lost except the one destined to be lost, so that the scripture might be fulfilled. ¹³ But now I am coming to you, and I speak these things in the world so that they may have my joy made complete in themselves.

"I am not asking on behalf of the world" (17:9). This may sound like a declaration of exclusive love. Does Jesus love only his disciples? In the context of the Gospel, it is clear that Jesus' love reaches out to all men and women. Recall the famous statement in John 3:16–17: "God so loved the world that he gave his only Son, so that everyone who believes in him may not perish but may have eternal life. Indeed, God did not send the Son into the world to condemn the world, but in order that the world might be saved through him." Although he now prays in a special way for those who have believed in him, he is about to demonstrate his love for all men and women by carrying his cross to Golgotha to die for all. Jesus' love for all men and women is indicated here by the fact that he is leaving his disciples "in the world" (17:11) so that they can carry on the mission that he has begun. Soon he will send them out to give all people the opportunity to enter into his life (20:21–23).

Nevertheless, while the rest of humanity is not excluded from his love, Jesus does focus here on his disciples. As the divine Word made flesh, Jesus embodies the Father's love. During his earthly life, he has made the Father's love present to the disciples simply by his presence with them. Now he prays that they may continue to be in his presence—that they may continue to be in union with him. The world, Jesus foresees, will often be hostile to us, his disciples. And we will be weak—susceptible to fear and vulnerable to temptations. So he prays for our protection.

God will give us his protection by drawing us into his "name," that is, into himself (17:11, 12). By praying this petition aloud while his disciples listen, Jesus lets them know of his concern for their protection. Being assured of his care, we can set aside anxiety and share in his joy (17:13).

¹⁴ I have given them your word, and the world has hated them because they do not belong to the world, just as I do not belong to the world. ¹⁵ I am not asking you to take them out of the world, but I ask you to protect them from the evil one. ¹⁶ They do not belong to the world, just as I do not belong to the world. ¹⁷ Sanctify them in the truth; your word is truth. ¹⁸ As you have sent me into the world, so I have sent them into the world. ¹⁹ And for their sakes I sanctify myself, so that they also may be sanctified in truth.

By saying that we do not "belong to the world," Jesus is not suggesting that he wants us to try to keep safe from the forces of evil in society by huddling together in a Christian ghetto. He sends us into the world for the sake of people in it. But he does not want us to derive our basic identity from the world around us, any more than he derives his basic identity from the world. He identifies himself as the Son of God, and he has come to share that identity with us (1:12; 20:17). Thus we are to be in the world (17:18), in the sense of being on earth and participating in society, but we are not to belong to the world (17:14), in the sense of participating in attitudes and behavior that are at odds with God's will.

Here Jesus uses another word that is not part of everyday speech: *sanctify* (17:17, 19). In the Old Testament, the term often translated "sanctify" refers to dedicating people and things to God's service. Sometimes the term is translated "consecrate," in the sense of taking something out of ordinary use and devoting it to God's service (Deuteronomy 15:19–21). Here, being "sanctified in truth" (17:19) means being drawn into a personal relationship with God through Jesus' cleansing word (see 15:3). Jesus asks God to set us aside for his service in the world. So that this can happen, Jesus sets himself aside for God's service in the most profound way: he offers his life to God as a sacrifice on our behalf (17:19).

In his teaching and activities, Jesus has revealed God's love and has challenged people to believe in him. After his death and resurrection, he will continue this mission of revelation and challenge through his disciples (17:18).

Finally, Jesus prays for disciples yet to come.

While Jesus has implicitly been praying for us—his future disciples—throughout his prayer, here he speaks of us explicitly.

20 I ask not only on behalf of these, but also on behalf of those who will believe in me through their word, 21 that they may all be one. As you, Father, are in me and I am in you, may they also be in us, so that the world may believe that you have sent me. 22 The glory that you have given me I have given them, so that they may be one, as we are one, 23 I in them and you in me, that they may become completely one, so that the world may know that you have sent me and have loved them even as you have loved me. 24 Father, I desire that those also, whom you have given me, may be with me where I am, to see my glory, which you have given me because you loved me before the foundation of the world.

25 Righteous Father, the world does not know you, but I know you; and these know that you have sent me. 26 I made your name known to them, and I will make it known, so that the love with which you have loved me may be in them, and I in them.

Jesus asks the Father to make us into a community—one in mind and heart. "May all be one," he prays, "as you, Father, are in me and I am in you" (17:21). Jesus is holding up the unity of Father and Son as the model for us to imitate. Yet, obviously, by ourselves we can hardly imitate the unity of the divine Persons. We can reflect the unity of the Father and the Son only by *sharing* in their unity. And it is precisely for this that Jesus prays. "As you, Father, are in me and I am in you, may they also be in us" (17:21). The Father has loved us as he has loved his only Son (17:23, 26). As a result, we can grow in love for one another as a small human expression of the infinite love of God.

Notice that Jesus expects his unity with the Father to be manifested in us here and now, in our present, earthly life. He wants us to become "completely one, so that the world may know" that the Father has sent him into the world (17:23). As Jesus said at the beginning of the Last Supper, "By this all will identify you as my disciples—by the love you show for one another" (see 13:35).

This unity is primarily something that God brings about in us—if we cooperate. By letting us overhear his prayer to the Father, Jesus lets us know how important it is to him that we be united with one another.

Jesus' final plea is that we would ultimately be with him in the glory of the Father (17:24). The author of the first letter of John points out that reaching this goal involves a process of personal transformation, by God's grace. In order to see Jesus as he is, we must become like him (1 John 3:2).

Jesus falls silent. His prayer completed, he goes out with his disciples to meet his betrayer and death. Yet his final prayer does not fade into history. In his Last Supper prayer, Jesus expressed the purposes of his death: that we would share in the life of God, that God would be glorified, that God's love would be revealed in the world, and that we would make our way home safely to the glory he has in store for us. Now that he has laid down his life and has risen from the dead, Jesus continues to pray in heaven for these purposes to be fulfilled. "He is still our priest, our advocate who always pleads our cause," declares a preface for the Mass of Easter in the Roman rite. New Testament writers speak of Jesus as the eternal intercessor (Hebrews 7:25; 1 John 2:1). John 17 gives us an insight into his eternal intercession.

New Testament scholar Rudolph Schnackenburg pointed out that Jesus' Last Supper prayer is, "to be sure, an intercession by Jesus for the disciples, but at the same time it is an encouragement to pray in the same spirit to the Father. At another place he promises them: On that day when he is with the Father, he will no longer pray for them, for the Father himself loves them and will hear them (John 16:26–27)." Thus, while Jesus continues to pray for us to the Father, he invites us to pray with him. We do this, as his followers, whenever we pray for ourselves and others. Above all, we do it in the Eucharist. In every celebration of the Eucharist, we offer Jesus to the Father as the one perfect offering that removes sins and brings eternal life. We join him as he offers himself for the very purposes for which he prayed at the Last Supper.

Thus the eucharistic prayers of liturgies from both the Western and the Eastern branches of the Church echo the petitions of Jesus' Last Supper prayer. A few examples:

♦ Jesus' plea that his disciples "may all be one. As you, Father, are in me and I am in you, may they also be in us" (17:21) resounds in the Byzantine liturgy's appeal to God "that we, with one voice and one heart, may glorify and praise your most honored and sublime name, Father, Son, and Holy Spirit, now and ever and forever."

♦ Jesus' prayer "Holy Father, protect them in your name that you have given me" (17:11) echoes in the cry of the Chaldean liturgy: "Lord God, we are your weak and humble people who are gathered in your name and stand before you at this moment. We have received through tradition the example of your Son. Therefore, it is with joy, praise, and exultation that we remember this great, revered, holy, life-giving, and divine mystery which is the memorial of the passion, death, burial, and resurrection of our Lord and Savior Jesus Christ."

♦ Jesus' prayer "Father, I desire that those also, whom you have given me, may be with me where I am, to see my glory, which you have given me because you loved me before the foundation of the world" (17:24) is taken up in the Roman liturgy in Eucharistic Prayer II:

> Remember our brothers and sisters
> who have gone to their rest
> in the hope of rising again;
> bring them and all the departed
> into the light of your presence.
> Have mercy on us all;
> Make us worthy to share eternal life
> With Mary, the virgin Mother of God,
> With the apostles, and with all the saints
> Who have done your will throughout the ages.
> May we praise you in union with them,
> And give you glory
> Through your Son, Jesus Christ.

Jesus raised his eyes in prayer at the Last Supper and gazed
into the face of his Father (17:1). In doing so, he not only gave us
a glimpse of his relationship with the Father; he united us with
himself, so that we may share his vision of the Father. This we do
every time we participate in the re-presentation of his death and
resurrection in the Eucharist. We share in Jesus' offering of himself
to the Father and gaze with him into the face of the Father who
loves us. Thus we begin to experience the realization of Jesus'
prayer to his Father "that the love with which you have loved me may
be in them, and I in them" (17:26).

Suggestions for Bible Discussion Groups

L ike a camping trip, a Bible discussion group works best if you agree on where you're going and how you intend to get there. Many groups use their first meeting to talk over such questions. Here is a checklist of issues, with bits of advice from people who have experience in Bible discussions. (A planning discussion will go more smoothly if the leaders have thought through the following issues beforehand.)

Agree on your purpose. Are you getting together to gain wisdom and direction for your lives? to finally get acquainted with the Bible? to support one another in following Christ? to encourage those who are exploring—or reexploring—the Church? for other reasons?

Agree on attitudes. For example: "We're all beginners here." "We're here to help one another understand and respond to God's word." "We're not here to offer counseling or direction to one another." "We want to read Scripture prayerfully." What do *you* wish to emphasize? Make it explicit!

Agree on ground rules. Barbara J. Fleischer, in her useful book *Facilitating for Growth*, recommends that a group clearly state its approach to the following:

- *Preparation.* Do we agree to read the material and prepare answers to the questions before each meeting?
- *Attendance.* What kind of priority will we give to our meetings?
- *Self-revelation.* Are we willing to help the others in the group gradually get to know us—our weaknesses as well as our strengths, our needs as well as our gifts?
- *Listening.* Will we commit ourselves to listen to one another?
- *Confidentiality.* Will we keep everything that is shared *with* the group *in* the group?
- *Discretion.* Will we refrain from sharing about the faults and sins of people who are not in the group?
- *Encouragement and support.* Will we give as well as receive?
- *Participation.* Will we give each person the time and opportunity to make a contribution?

You could probably take a pen and draw a circle around
listening and *confidentiality*. Those two points are especially
important.

The following items could be added to Fleischer's list:

♦ *Relationship with parish.* Is our group part of the adult faith-
formation program? independent but operating with the
express approval of the pastor? not a parish-based group?

♦ *New members.* Will we let new members join us once we have
begun the six weeks of discussions?

Agree on housekeeping.

♦ *When will we meet?*

♦ *How often will we meet?* Meeting weekly or every other week
is best if you can manage it. William Riley remarks, "Meetings
once a month are too distant from each other for the threads
of the last session not to be lost" (*The Bible Study Group: An
Owner's Manual*).

♦ *How long will each meeting run?*

♦ *Where will we meet?*

♦ *Is any setup needed?* Christine Dodd writes that "the problem
with meeting in a place like a church hall is that it can be
very soul-destroying," given the cold, impersonal feel of many
church facilities. If you have to meet in a church facility,
Dodd recommends doing something to make the area homey
(*Making Scripture Work*).

♦ *Who will host the meetings?* Leaders and hosts are not
necessarily the same people.

♦ *Will we have refreshments?* Who will provide them? Don
Cousins and Judson Poling make this recommendation: "Serve
refreshments if you like, but save snacks and other foods for
the end of the meeting to minimize distractions" (*Leader's
Guide 1*).

♦ *What about child care?* Most experienced leaders of Bible
discussion groups discourage bringing infants or other children
to adult Bible discussions.

Agree on leadership. You need someone to facilitate—
to keep the discussion on track, to see that everyone has a chance

to speak, to help the group stay on schedule. Rena Duff, editor of the newsletter *Sharing God's Word Today*, recommends having two or three people take turns leading the discussions.

It's okay if the leader is not an expert on the Bible. You have this Six Weeks book as a guide, and if questions come up that no one can answer, you can delegate a participant to do a little research between meetings. Perhaps your parish priest or someone on the pastoral staff of your parish could offer advice. Or help may be available from your diocesan catechetical office or a local Catholic college or seminary.

It's important for the leader to set an example of listening, to draw out the quieter members (and occasionally restrain the more vocal ones), to move the group on when it gets stuck, to get the group back on track when the discussion moves away from the topic, and to restate and summarize what the group is learning. Sometimes the leader needs to remind the members of their agreements. An effective group leader is enthusiastic about the topic and the discussions and sets an example of learning from others and of using resources for growing in understanding.

As a discussion group matures, other members of the group will increasingly share in doing all these things on their own initiative.

Bible discussion is an opportunity to experience the fulfillment of Jesus' promise "Where two or three are gathered in my name, I am there among them" (Matthew 18:20). Put your discussion group in Jesus' hands. Pray for the guidance of the Spirit. And have a great time exploring God's word together!

Suggestions for Individuals

Y ou can use this book just as well for individual study as for group discussion. While discussing the Bible with other people can be a rich experience, there are advantages to reading on your own. For example:

♦ You can focus on the points that interest you most.

♦ You can go at your own pace.

♦ You can be completely relaxed and unashamedly honest in your answers to all the questions, since you don't have to share them with anyone!

My suggestions for using this book on your own are these:

♦ Don't skip "Questions to Begin." The questions can help you as an individual reader warm up to the topic of the reading.

♦ Take your time on "Questions for Careful Reading" and "Questions for Application." While a group will probably not have enough time to work on all the questions, you can allow yourself the time to consider all of them if you are using the book by yourself.

♦ After reading "Guide to the Reading," go back and reread the Scripture text before answering the Questions for Application.

♦ Take the time to look up all the parenthetical Scripture references in the introduction, the Guides to the Reading, and the other material.

♦ Since you control the pace, give yourself plenty of opportunities to reflect on the meaning of the Scripture passages for you. Let your reading be an opportunity for these words to become God's words to you.

Resources

Bibles

The following editions of the Bible contain the full set of biblical books recognized by the Catholic Church, along with a great deal of useful explanatory material:

♦ The Catholic Study Bible (Oxford University Press), which uses the text of the New American Bible
♦ The Catholic Bible: Personal Study Edition (Oxford University Press), which also uses the text of the New American Bible
♦ The New Jerusalem Bible, the regular (not the reader's) edition (Doubleday)

Books, Web Sites, and Other Resources

♦ Robert J. Karris, *Prayer and the New Testament* (New York: Crossroad, 2000).
♦ George Martin, *Praying with Jesus* (Chicago: Loyola Press, 2000).

How has Scripture had an impact on your life? Was this book helpful to you in your study of the Bible? Please send comments, suggestions, and personal experiences to Kevin Perrotta, General Editor, Editorial Department, Loyola Press, 3441 N. Ashland Ave., Chicago, IL 60657.